AUTOMATION AND THE FUTURE OF WORK

AUTOMATION AND THE FUTURE OF WORK

Aaron Benanav

VERSO

London • New York

First published by Verso 2020
© Aaron Benanav 2020

An earlier version of this text appeared as "Automation and the Future of Work,"
New Left Review, nos. 119, Sept.–Oct. 2019 and 120, Nov.–Dec. 2019.

1 3 5 7 9 10 8 6 4 2

Verso
UK: 6 Meard Street, London W1F 0EG
US: 20 Jay Street, Suite 1010, Brooklyn, NY 11201
versobooks.com

Verso is the imprint of New Left Books

ISBN-13: 978-1-83976-129-4
ISBN-13: 978-1-83976-130-0 (UK EBK)
ISBN-13: 978-1-83976-131-7 (US EBK)

British Library Cataloguing in Publication Data
A catalogue record for this book is available from the British Library

Library of Congress Cataloging-in-Publication Data
A catalog record for this book is available from the Library of Congress

Typeset in Garamond by Hewer Text UK Ltd, Edinburgh
Printed and bound by CPI Group (UK) Ltd, Croydon CR0 4YY

Contents

Figures

Tables

Preface

THE INTERNET, SMARTPHONES, AND social media have already transformed so much about the way we interact with each other and come to know the world. What would happen if these digital technologies moved off the screen and increasingly integrated themselves into the physical world around us? Advanced industrial robotics, self-driving cars and trucks, and intelligent cancer-screening machines appear to presage a world of ease, but they also make us uneasy. After all, what would *human beings* do in a largely automated future? Would we be able to adapt our institutions to realize the dream of human freedom that a new age of intelligent machines might make possible? Or would that dream turn out to be a nightmare of mass technological unemployment?

In two *New Left Review* articles published in 2019, I identified a new automation discourse propounded by liberal, right-wing, and left analysts alike. Asking just these sorts of questions, automation theorists arrive at a provocative conclusion: mass technological unemployment is coming and can be managed only by the provision of universal basic income, since large sections of the population will lose access to the wages they need to survive.

In this book, I argue that the resurgence of the automation discourse today is a response to a real trend unfolding across the world: there are simply too few jobs for too many people. This chronic labor underdemand is manifest in economic trends such as jobless recoveries, stagnant wages, and rampant job insecurity. It is visible as well in the political phenomena that rising inequality catalyzes: populism, plutocracy, and the rise of a new, sea-steading digital elite—more focused on escaping in rockets to Mars than on improving the livelihoods of the digital peasantry who will be left behind on a burning planet Earth.

Pointing with one hand to the homeless and jobless masses of Oakland, California, and with the other to the robots staffing the Tesla production plant just a few miles away in Fremont, it is easy to believe that the automation theorists must be right. However, the explanation they offer—that runaway technological change is destroying jobs—is simply false. There is a real and persistent underdemand for labor in the United States and European Union, and even more so in countries such as South Africa, India, and Brazil, yet its cause is almost the opposite of the one identified by the automation theorists.

In reality, rates of labor-productivity growth are slowing down, not speeding up. That should have increased the demand for labor, except that the productivity slowdown was overshadowed by another, more eventful trend: in a development originally analyzed by Marxist economist Robert Brenner under the title of the "long downturn"—and belatedly recognized by mainstream economists as "secular stagnation" or "Japanification"—economies have been growing at a progressively slower pace. The cause? Decades of industrial overcapacity killed the manufacturing growth engine, and no alternative to it has been found, least of all in the slow-growing, low-productivity activities that make up the bulk of the service sector.

As economic growth decelerates, rates of job creation slow, and it is this, not technology-induced job destruction, that has depressed the global demand for labor. Put on the reality-vision glasses of John Carpenter's *They Live*, which allowed the protagonist of that film to see the truth in advertising, and it is easy to see a world not of shiny new automated factories and ping-pong-playing consumer robots, but of crumbling infrastructures, deindustrialized cities, harried nurses, and underpaid salespeople, as well as a massive stock of financialized capital with dwindling places to invest itself.

In an effort to revive stagnant economies, governments spent almost a half century imposing punishing austerity on their populations, underfunding schools, hospitals, public transportation networks, and welfare programs. At the same time, in a world of ultralow interest rates, governments, businesses, and households took on record quantities of debt. They did not do so to invest in our digital future, as former Federal Reserve chairman Alan Greenspan argued they would in the midst of the late-1990s tech bubble. Instead, firms mortgaged their assets to pay off shareholders, while poorer households borrowed in an effort to make ends meet.

These trends have left the world economy in an incredibly poor position as it faces one of its greatest challenges: the COVID-19 recession. Dilapidated healthcare systems have been overrun with patients, and schools have closed that were for many children vital sources of basic nutrition (and for parents, of much-needed childcare). Meanwhile, the economy is tanking. Heavily indebted companies watched their stock values plummet, at least initially, at rates not seen since the Great Depression. Unemployment rates rose significantly across the world, and stratospherically in the United States, leaving large parts of the population unable to pay for food, medical care, or housing. In spite of massive monetary and fiscal stimuli, weak economies are unlikely to bounce back quickly from the shock. It is easy to see how over the long term, the COVID-19 recession will accelerate what are by now long-unfolding trends of rising economic insecurity and inequality.

It is precisely for this reason that it is so important to reflect on today's automation discourse. Automation theorists offer a utopian reply to our dystopian world. Remove the *They Live* reality-vision glasses and return for a moment to the world of fantasy inhabited by these authors. In it, we all work less (like the victims of the present recession) yet have access to everything we need to make a life; we spend more time with our families (but not because we are in imposed isolation); the elderly jog through parks wearing new exoskeleton jumpsuits (rather than dying in hospital beds); and the air has been cleared of smog because we are transitioning rapidly to a world of renewable energy (rather than because factories have been shuttered and people are no longer driving cars). With the exception of the exoskeleton jumpsuits, all of this is possible now if we fight for it. We can already achieve the post-scarcity world that the automation theorists invoke, even if the automation of production proves impossible.

My interest in this topic arose from two distinct sources, one in the deeper past and the other more recent. Like many of the automation theorists, I grew up in the 1980s and '90s reading science fiction novels and watching the spacefaring communists of *Star Trek: The Next Generation* tour the galaxy. My father, who inspired these interests, was himself a researcher in the field of automation. Like many of his peers, he left a career in academia to try his luck in the startup culture of the 1990s. Some people made a lot of money in those years, but many more did not: most internet startups went bust, leaving their overworked engineers with little to show for their efforts. Interning with him at a different company every summer of high school—writing HTML and Javascript—I decided that there was little promise of happiness to be found in the digital economy, so I devoted myself instead to studying the history of economic growth and unemployment, the twin engines of prosperity and insecurity in the contemporary economy.

In the aftermath of the 2008 crisis, I became involved in the social movements of my time, an experience I attempted to digest through conversation and collaboration with fellow members of the *Endnotes* collective. The unsigned, coauthored texts we wrote have greatly influenced the analysis to be found in these pages. It was through an encounter with two critics—Nick Srnicek and Alex Williams, whose *Inventing the Future* (2015) is a key example of the left wing of the automation discourse—that I discovered the intellectual ecosystem populated by the automation theorists, which led me back to my childhood love of science fiction and at the same time transformed my outlook on the future.

As I read book after book by the automation theorists, supplementing that still-growing reading list with forays into the utopian and science fiction literatures of the past, the conviction grew within me that, collectively, these authors had done more than anyone I have yet encountered to think through the logical organization of a post-capitalist society and to imagine the pathways by which we might get there. I disagreed with their analysis of the present but saw responding to their vision of the future as a way to develop my own, which by comparison with theirs was still of the dullest-possible grey. In the pages that follow, I explore possibilities for achieving a post-scarcity future without the full automation of production: by sharing the work that remains to be done in a way that restores dignity, autonomy, and purpose to working life without making work the center of our shared, social existence.

In the course of an exposition and critique of the automation discourse, I lay out a brief history of what has happened to the world economy and its workforce over the past fifty years, focusing on the origins and development of the present-day, chronically low demand for labor. I discuss the policy alternatives that aim to resolve this market failure—neoliberal structural adjustment, Keynesian demand management, and universal basic income—and sketch out a post-scarcity world against which they should be measured.

Writing this book has only further convinced me that turning the tide toward a more humane future will depend on the refusal of masses of working people to accept a persistent decline in the demand for their labor and the rising economic inequality it entails. Struggles against these outcomes were unfolding with increasing intensity across the globe before the COVID-19 recession, and have recently resurged. We need to immerse ourselves in the movements born of these struggles, helping to drive them forward. If they fail, maybe the best we will get is a slightly higher social wage in the form of universal basic income—a proposal governments are now testing out as a possible response to the present recession. We should not be fighting for this modest social goal, but rather to inaugurate a post-scarcity planet.

I could not have written this book without the support and friendship of many people, including: Perry Anderson, Arielle Angel, Elyse Arkind, Marc Arkind, Mia Beach, Dan Benanav, Ethan Benanav, Mandy Benanav, Jasper Bernes, Mårten Björk, Jan Breman, J. Dakota Brown, Jonny Bunning, Paul Cheney, Christopher Chitty (RIP), Joshua Clover, Chiara Cordelli, Oliver Cussen, Daniel Denvir, Andreas Eckert, Hugh Farrell, Adom Getachew, Maya Gonzalez, Daragh Grant, Lee Harris, Gary Herrigel, Joel Isaac, Felix Kurz, Rachel Kushner, Natalie Leonard, Jonathan Levy, Marcel van der Linden, Rob Lucas, Neil Maclean, Henry Mulheim, Jeanne Neton, Mary Ellen O'Brien, Chris O'Kane, Moishe Postone (RIP), Thea Riafrancos, Pavlos Roufos, Bill Sewell, Jason Smith, Maureen Smyth, Juliana Spahr, Zöe Sutherland, Ben Tarnoff, Sarah Watlington, Suzi Weissman, Björn Westergard, Gabriel Winant, and Daniel Zamora, as well as participants in the History and Theory of Capitalism Workshop and the Society of Fellows Workshop, both at the University of Chicago. I am especially grateful to Chloe Benanav, Robert Brenner, John Clegg, and Charlotte Robertson, who supported me in my research and writing every step of the way. Lastly, thank you to my editors at the *New Left Review*, Susan Watkins, Tom Hazeldine, Emma Fajgenbaum, and Lola Seaton, and at Verso, Tom Hazeldine (again), Duncan Ranslem, and Sam Smith. Thanks especially to Tom, who pushed this project along an accelerated timeline despite a world turned upside down.

This book is dedicated to my wife, Chloe, with whom I have tasted the good life.

Aaron Benanav
Chicago, June 2020

CHAPTER 1

The Automation Discourse

RAPID ADVANCES IN ARTIFICIAL intelligence, machine learning, and robotics seem set to transform the world of work. In the most advanced factories in the world, companies like Tesla are pushing toward "lights out" production, in which fully automated work processes, no longer needing human hands, can run in the dark. Meanwhile, in the illuminated halls of robotics conventions, machines are on display that can play ping-pong, cook food, have sex, and even hold conversations. Computers are not only generating new strategies for playing Go but are said to be writing symphonies that will bring audiences to tears. Dressed in white lab coats or donning virtual suits, computers are learning to identify cancers and will soon be put to work developing legal strategies. Trucks are already barreling across the United States without drivers; robotic dogs are carrying military-grade weapons across desolate plains. Are we living in the last days of human toil? Is what Edward Bellamy once called the "edict of Eden" about to be revoked, as "men"—or at least, the wealthiest among us—become like gods?[1]

There are many reasons to doubt the hype. For one thing, machines remain comically incapable of opening doors or, alas, folding laundry. Robotic security guards are toppling into mall fountains. Computerized digital assistants can answer questions and translate documents, but not well enough to do the job without human intervention; the same is true of self-driving cars.[2] In 2014, in the midst of the American "Fight for Fifteen" movement, billboards went up in San Francisco threatening to replace fast-food workers with touchscreens if a law raising the minimum wage were passed. The *Wall Street Journal* dubbed the bill the "robot employment act." Yet many fast-food workers in Europe already work alongside touchscreens, often earning better pay than comparable workers in the United States.[3] So is the talk of automation overblown?

In the pages of newspapers and popular magazines, scare stories about automation remain just so much idle chatter. However, over the past decade, this talk has crystalized into an influential social theory that purports not only to analyze current technologies and predict their future, but also to explore the consequences of technological change for society at large. The automation discourse rests on four principal propositions. First, it argues, workers are already being displaced by ever more advanced machines, resulting in rising levels of "technological unemployment." Second, this displacement is a sure sign that we are on the verge of achieving a largely automated society, in which nearly all work will be performed by self-moving machines and intelligent computers. Third, although automation should entail humanity's collective liberation from toil, we live in a society where most people must work in order to live, meaning this dream may well turn out to be a nightmare.[4] Fourth, therefore, the only way to prevent a mass-unemployment catastrophe—like the one unfolding in the United States in 2020, although for very different reasons—is to institute a universal basic income (UBI), breaking the connection between the size of the incomes people earn and the amount of work they do.

The Machines Are Coming

Self-described futurists are the major disseminators of this automation discourse. In the widely read *Second Machine Age*, Erik Brynjolfsson and Andrew McAfee argue that we find ourselves "at an inflection point—a bend in the curve where many technologies that used to be found only in science fiction are becoming everyday reality." New technologies promise an enormous "bounty," but, Brynjolfsson and McAfee caution, "there is no economic law that says that all workers, or even a majority of workers, will benefit from these advances." On the contrary: as the demand for labor falls with the adoption of more advanced technologies, wages are stagnating; a rising share of annual income is therefore being captured by capital rather than by labor. The result is growing inequality, which could "slow our journey" into what they call a new "machine age" by generating a "failure mode of capitalism" in which rentier extraction crowds out technological innovation.[5] In *Rise of the Robots*, Martin Ford similarly claims that we are pushing "towards a tipping point" that is poised to "make the entire economy less labour-intensive." Again, "the most frightening long-term scenario of all might be if the global economic system eventually manages to adapt to the new reality," leading to the creation of an "automated feudalism" in which the "peasants would be largely superfluous" and the elite impervious to economic demands.[6] For these authors, education and retraining will not be enough to stabilize labor demand in an automated economy; some form of guaranteed nonwage income, such as a negative income tax, must be put in place.[7]

This automation discourse has been enthusiastically adopted by the jeans-wearing elite of Silicon Valley. Bill Gates advocated for a robots tax. Mark Zuckerberg told Harvard undergraduate inductees to "explore ideas like universal basic income," a policy Elon Musk also thinks will become increasingly "necessary" over time, as robots outcompete humans across a growing range of jobs.[8] Musk gave his SpaceX drone vessels names like "Of Course I Still Love You" and "Just Read the Instructions," which he lifted from the names of spaceships in Iain M. Banks's *Culture* series. Banks's ambiguously utopian science fiction novels depict a post-scarcity world in which human beings live fulfilling lives alongside intelligent robots—called "minds"—without the need for markets or states.[9]

Politicians and their advisors have equally identified with the automation discourse, which has become one of the leading perspectives on our "digital future." In his farewell presidential address, Barack Obama suggested that the "next wave of economic dislocations" will come not from overseas trade, but rather from "the relentless pace of automation that makes a lot of good, middle-class jobs obsolete." Robert Reich, former labor secretary under Bill Clinton, expressed similar fears: we will soon reach a point "where technology is displacing so many jobs, not just menial jobs but also professional jobs, that we're going to have to take seriously the notion of a universal basic income." Clinton's former Treasury secretary, Lawrence Summers, made the same admission: once-"stupid" ideas about technological unemployment now seem increasingly smart, he said, as workers' wages stagnate and economic inequality rises. The discourse even became the basis of a long-shot presidential campaign for 2020: Andrew Yang, Obama's former "Ambassador of Global Entrepreneurship," penned his own tome on automation titled *The War on Normal People* and ran a futuristic campaign on a "Humanity First" platform, introducing UBI into mainstream American politics for the first time in two generations. Among Yang's supporters was Andy Stern, former head of the Service Employees International Union (SEIU), whose *Raising the Floor* is yet another example of the discourse.[10]

Yang and Stern—like all of the other writers named so far—take pains to assure readers that some variant of capitalism is here to stay, even if it must jettison its labor markets; however, they admit to the influence of figures on the far left who offer a more radical version of the automation discourse. In *Inventing the Future*, Nick Srnicek and Alex Williams argue that the "most recent wave of automation is poised" to transform the labor market "drastically, as it comes to encompass every aspect of the economy."[11] They claim that only a socialist government would actually be able to fulfill the promise of full automation by creating a post-work or post-scarcity society. In *Four Futures*, Peter Frase thoughtfully explores the alternative outcomes for such a post-scarcity society, depending on whether it were still to have private property or to suffer from resource scarcity, both of which could persist even if labor scarcity were overcome.[12]

Like the liberal proponents of the automation discourse, these left-wing writers stress that even if the coming of advanced robotics is inevitable, "there is no necessary progression into a post-work world."[13] Srnicek, Williams, and Frase are all proponents of UBI, but in a left-wing variant. For them, UBI serves as a bridge to "fully automated luxury communism," a term Aaron Bastani coined in 2014 to name a possible goal of socialist politics. This term flourished for five years as a meme before Bastani's book—outlining an automated future in which artificial intelligence, solar power, gene editing, asteroid mining, and lab-grown meat generate a world of limitless leisure and self-invention—finally appeared.[14] It provided a much-needed counterweight to left-wing rhetorics of collective self-sacrifice and anti-consumerist austerity.

Recurrent Fears

These futurist visions, arising from all points along the political spectrum, depend upon a shared prediction about the trajectory of technological change. If anything, the confidence that is characteristic of the automation discourse has only increased in the midst of the pandemic recession. Although technological change was not itself the cause of job loss—at least this time around—automation theorists argue that the spread of the pandemic will hasten the transition to a more automated future. Lost jobs will never return since, unlike their human counterparts, cooking, cleaning, recycling, grocery-bagging, and caretaking robots can neither catch COVID-19 nor transmit it to others.[15] Have the automation theorists got this story right?

To answer this question, it is helpful to have a couple of working definitions. Automation may be distinguished from other forms of labor-saving technical innovation in that automation technologies *fully substitute* for human labor, rather than merely augmenting human productive capacities. With labor-augmenting technologies, a given job category will continue to exist, but each worker in that category will be more productive. For example, the addition of new machines to a car assembly line will make line work more efficient without abolishing line work as such; fewer line workers will be needed in total to produce any given number of automobiles. Whether such technical change results in job destruction depends on the relative speeds of productivity and output growth in the automotive industry: if output grows more slowly than labor productivity—a common case, as we will see below—then the number of jobs will decline. This is true even without automation entering the picture. By contrast, true automation takes place, as Kurt Vonnegut suggested in his novel *Player Piano*, whenever an entire "job classification has been eliminated. Poof."[16] No matter how much production increases, there will never be another telephone switchboard operator or hand manipulator of rolled steel. Here, machines have fully substituted for human labor.

Much of the debate around the future of workplace automation turns, unhelpfully, on an evaluation of the degree to which present or near-future technologies are labor-substituting or labor-augmenting in character. Distinguishing between these two types of technical change is more difficult than one might suppose. When a retailer installs four self-checkout machines, watched over and periodically adjusted by a single employee, has cashiering ended as an occupation, or is each cashier now operating three additional registers? Taking an extreme view on such issues, one famous study from the Oxford Martin School suggested that 47 percent of jobs in the United States are at high risk of automation; a more recent study from the Organisation for Economic Co-operation and Development (OECD) predicts that 14 percent of jobs are at high risk, with another 32 percent at risk of significant change in the way they are carried out—due to innovations that augment labor rather than substitute for it.[17]

In fact, both types of technical change can be expected to leave many workers without jobs. It is unclear, however, whether even the highest of these estimates suggests a qualitative break with the past has taken place. By one count, "57 per cent of the jobs workers did in the 1960s no longer exist today."[18] Alongside other forms of technical change, automation has been a persistent source of job loss over time. The question I address here is not whether new automation technologies will destroy additional jobs in the future (the answer is certainly yes). It is whether these technologies—advanced robotics, artificial intelligence, and machine learning—have so accelerated the rate of job destruction and so diminished the rate of new job creation that increasing numbers of people are already finding themselves permanently unemployed.

If so, that would completely upend the normal functioning of capitalist economies. This insight, on which the automation theory is based, was stated most succinctly by Nobel Prize–winning economist Wassily Leontief in 1983. The "effective operation of the automatic price mechanism," he explained, "depends critically" on a peculiar feature of modern technology, namely that in spite of bringing about "an unprecedented rise in total output," it nevertheless "strengthened the dominant role of human labour in most kinds of productive processes."[19] In other words, technology has made workers more productive without making work itself unnecessary. Since workers continue to earn wages, their demand for goods is effective. At any time, a technological breakthrough could destroy this fragile pin holding capitalist societies together. Artificial general intelligence, for example, might eliminate many occupations in a single stroke, rendering large quantities of labor unsalable at any price. At that point, information about the preferences of large sections of the population would vanish from the market, rendering it inoperable. Drawing on this insight—and adding that such a breakthrough now exists—automation theorists frequently argue that capitalism must be a transitory mode of production, which will give way to a new form of life that does not organize itself around wage work and monetary exchange.[20]

Automation may be a constant feature of capitalist societies; the same is not true of the theory of a coming age of automation, which extrapolates from instances of technological change to a broader account of social transformation. On the contrary, its recurrence in modern history has been periodic. Excitement about a coming age of automation can be traced back to at least the mid nineteenth century, with the publication of Charles Babbage's *On the Economy of Machinery and Manufactures* in 1832, John Adolphus Etzler's *The Paradise within the Reach of All Men, without Labour* in 1833, and Andrew Ure's *The Philosophy of Manufactures* in 1835. These books

presaged the imminent emergence of largely or fully automated factories, run with minimal or merely supervisory human labor. Their
vision was a major influence on Marx, whose *Capital* argued that a
complex world of interacting machines was in the process of displacing human labor from the center of economic life.[21]

Visions of automated factories appeared again in the 1930s, 1950s,
and 1980s, before reemerging in the 2010s. Each time, they were
accompanied or shortly followed by predictions of a coming age of
"catastrophic unemployment and social breakdown," which could be
prevented only if society were reorganized.[22] To point out the periodicity of this discourse is not to say that its accompanying social
visions should be dismissed. For one thing, the technological breakthroughs presaged by the automation discourse could still be achieved
at any time. Just because they were wrong in the past does not necessarily mean that they will always be wrong in the future. More than
that, these visions of automation have clearly been generative in social
terms: they point to certain utopian possibilities latent within capitalist societies. Indeed, some of the most visionary socialists of the
twentieth century either were automation theorists or were inspired
by them, including Herbert Marcuse, James Boggs, and André Gorz.

Taking its periodicity into account, automation theory may be
described as a spontaneous discourse of capitalist societies that, for a
mixture of structural and contingent reasons, reappears in those societies time and again as a way of thinking through their limits. What
summons the automation discourse periodically into being is a deep
anxiety about the functioning of the labor market: there are simply
too few jobs for too many people. Why is the market unable to
provide jobs for so many of the workers who need them? Proponents
of the automation discourse explain this problem of a low demand for
labor in terms of runaway technological change.[23]

Too Few Jobs

If the automation discourse appeals so widely again today, it is
because the ascribed consequences of automation are all around us:

global capitalism *is* failing to provide jobs for many of the people who need them. There has been, in other words, a persistently low demand for labor, one which is no longer adequately registered in unemployment statistics.[24] Labor underdemand is reflected in higher spikes of unemployment during recessions, as in the 2020 pandemic recession, and in increasingly jobless recoveries, a phenomenon likely to be repeated in the pandemic recession's aftermath.[25] Low labor demand has been evident, as well, in a trend with more generic consequences for working people: a decline in the share of all income earned in a given year that is distributed as wages rather than profits.[26] Mainstream economists long held the steadiness of the labor share to be a stylized fact of economic growth, which was supposed to ensure that the gains of economic development were widely distributed. In spite of massive accumulations of so-called human capital, in the form of rising educational attainments and healthier lives, the labor share of income in G7 countries has fallen for decades (Figure 1.1).

Such shifts signal a radical reduction in workers' bargaining power. And the typical worker has faced harsher realities than even these statistics suggest, since wage growth has become increasingly skewed toward the highest earners: the infamous 1 percent. Growing gaps have not only widened between the average growth rates of labor productivity and of wages—which cumulatively causes the labor share of income to fall—but also between the growth rates of average wages and median wages—which evinces a shift in labor incomes from production and nonsupervisory workers toward managers and CEOs. The result is that many workers have seen a vanishingly thin slice of economic growth (Figure 1.2).[27] Under these conditions, rising economic inequality will be contained only by the strength of redistributive programs. However, the "politics of social solidarity" have been weakening over time.[28] Even critics of the automation discourse, such as economists David Autor and Robert J. Gordon, are disturbed by these trends: something has gone wrong with the economy, leading to a low demand for labor.[29]

Figure 1.1. Labor Share of Income, G7 Economies, 1980–2015

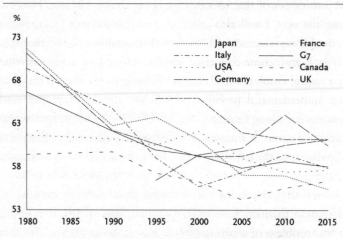

Source: OECD Compendium of Productivity Indicators, 2017, Chapter 1, Figure 1.8.

Figure 1.2. Productivity-Wages Gap, OECD Countries, 1995–2013

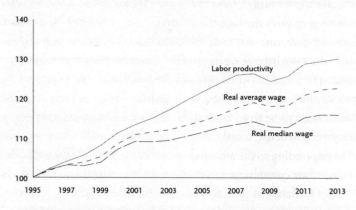

Note: 1995=100. Employment weighted average of twenty-four countries, including Finland, Germany, Japan, Korea, United States, France, Italy, Sweden, Austria, Belgium, UK, Australia, Spain, Czechia, Denmark, Hungary, Poland, Netherlands, Norway, Canada, New Zealand, Ireland, Israel and Slovakia. For detailed information, see the OECD Economic Outlook.
Source: OECD Economic Outlook, Volume 2018, Issue 2, Chapter 2, Figure 2.2.

Has runaway technological change been the cause of the low demand for labor, as proponents of the automation theory suggest? I will join critics of that theory in arguing that it has not. However, along the way, I will also criticize the critics—both for providing alternative explanations of a persistently low labor demand that apply only in high-income countries, and for failing to produce anything like a radical vision of social change adequate to the scale of the global labor underdemand problem, which has already beset the world economy for a long time and, due to COVID-19, is likely to worsen in years to come. It should be said from the outset that I am more sympathetic to the left wing of the automation discourse than to any of its critics.

Even if the explanation they offer turns out to be inadequate, the automation theorists have at least focused the world's attention on the real problem of a consistently low demand for labor. They have also excelled in efforts to imagine solutions to this problem that are broadly emancipatory in character. The automation theorists are our late-capitalist utopians.[30] In a world reeling from a global pandemic, rising inequality, recalcitrant neoliberalism, resurgent ethnonationalism, and the looming threat of climate change, automation theorists have tried to push through the catastrophe with a vision of an emancipated future, one in which humanity advances to the next stage in our history—whatever we might take that to mean—and technology helps to free us all to discover and follow our passions. That is true in spite of the fact that, as with many of the utopias of the past, these visions need to be freed from their authors' technocratic fantasies as to how constructive social change might take place.

In responding to the automation discourse, the following chapters advance four counterarguments. First, I argue that the decline in the demand for labor of past decades was due not to an unprecedented leap in technological innovation, but to ongoing technical change in an environment of deepening economic stagnation. Second, I contend that this underdemand for labor has tended to manifest not as mass unemployment but rather as persistent *underemployment*. Third, I point out that the resulting world of poorly paid workers will continue to be accepted or even welcomed by elites, meaning technological advances will by no means automatically entail the adoption of technocratic solutions like universal basic income (meanwhile, even if UBI is introduced, it is much more likely that it will prop up a world of massive inequality than help dismantle it). Fourth, I explain how we might create a world of abundance even without the full or nearly full automation of production. I then project a path by which we might get there, through social struggle rather than administrative intervention.

Historically, major shifts in social policy have been adopted only under massive pressure, such as the threat of communism or of civilizational collapse. Today, policy reforms could emerge in response to pressure coming from a new mass social movement, aiming to change the basic makeup of the social order. Instead of fearing that movement, we need to see ourselves as part of it, helping to articulate its goals and paths forward. If that movement is defeated, maybe the best we will get is UBI, but that distributional reform should not be our aim. We should be reaching toward a post-scarcity world, a goal that advanced technologies will help us realize, even if the full automation of production is not achievable—or even desirable.

The return of the automation discourse has been a symptom of our era, as it was in times past: it has arisen when the gap between the supply and demand for jobs becomes so large, leaving so many individuals scrambling to find scraps of work, that people begin to question the viability of a market-regulated society. Even prior to the outbreak of COVID-19, the breakdown of the labor-market mechanism was more extreme than at any time in the past. This is because, over the past half century, a greater share of the world's population than ever before came to depend on selling its labor (or the simple products of its labor) to survive in the context of weakening global economic growth rates. Our present reality is better described by near-future science fiction dystopias than by standard economic analysis; ours is a hot planet, with micro-drones flying over the heads of the street hawkers and rickshaw pullers, where the rich live in guarded, climate-controlled communities while the rest of us while away our time in dead-end jobs, playing video games on smartphones. We need to slip out of this timeline and into another.

A post-scarcity future—in which all individuals are guaranteed access to whatever they need to make a life, without exception—could become the basis on which humanity mounts a battle against climate change. It could also be the foundation on which we remake the world, creating the conditions in which, as James Boggs put it, "for the first time in human history, great masses of people will be free to explore and reflect, to question and to create, to learn and to teach, unhampered by the fear of where the next meal is coming from."[31] To find our way toward this post-scarcity future requires not only a break between work and income, as the automation theorists recognize, but also one between profit and income, as many do not.

Chapter 2

Labor's Global Deindustrialization

I F TECHNOLOGICALLY INDUCED JOB destruction is to have widespread social ramifications, it will have to eliminate employment in the service sector, which has absorbed 74 percent of workers in high-income countries and 52 percent worldwide.[1] Purveyors of the automation discourse therefore focus on "new forms of service-sector automation" in retail, transportation, and food services, where "robotization" is said to be "gathering steam" with a growing army of machines that take orders, stock shelves, drive cars, and flip burgers. Many more service sector jobs, including some that require years of education and training, will supposedly be rendered obsolete in the coming years due to advances in artificial intelligence.[2] Of course, these claims are mostly predictions about the effects that technologies will have on future patterns of employment. Such predictions can go wrong—as, for example, in the first week of January 2020, when three espresso-and-burger-slinging robotics firms in the Bay Area either closed or were forced to cut their losses.[3]

In making their case, automation theorists often point to the manufacturing sector as the precedent for what they imagine is beginning to happen in services. In manufacturing, the employment apocalypse has already taken place.[4] To evaluate these theorists' claims, it therefore makes sense to begin by looking at what role automation has played in that sector's fate. After all, manufacturing is the area most amenable to automation, since on the shop floor it is possible to "radically simplify the environment in which machines work, to enable autonomous operation."[5] Industrial robotics has been around for a long time: the first robot, the "Unimate," was installed in a General Motors plant in 1961. Still, until the late 1960s, scholars studying this sector were able to dismiss out of hand Luddite fears of long-term technological unemployment. Manufacturing employment grew most rapidly precisely in those lines where technical innovation was happening at the fastest pace, because it was in those lines that prices fell the fastest, stoking the growth of demand for products.[6] That era is long over. Over the past fifty years, industrialization has given way to deindustrialization, and not just in any one line, but across the manufacturing sectors of most countries.[7]

The Productivity Paradox

In the scholarly literature, deindustrialization is "most commonly defined as a decline in the share of manufacturing in total employment."[8] That share fell first of all across the high-income world, starting in the late 1960s and early 1970s. Manufacturing employed 22 percent of all workers in the United States in 1970, a share that declined to just 8 percent in 2017. Over the same period, manufacturing employment shares fell from 23 percent to 9 percent in France, and from 30 percent to 8 percent in the UK. Japan, Germany, and Italy experienced smaller but still-substantial declines: in Japan, from 25 percent to 15 percent; in Germany, from 29 percent to 17 percent; and in Italy, from 25 percent to 15 percent. In all cases, the declines were eventually associated with substantial falls in the total number of people employed in manufacturing. In the US, Germany, Italy, and Japan, the overall number of manufacturing jobs fell by approximately a third from postwar peaks; in France, it fell by 50 percent, and in the UK, by 67 percent.[9]

It is commonly assumed that deindustrialization in these high-income countries must be the result of production facilities moving offshore. Offshoring has certainly contributed to deindustrialization in the United States and UK, which boast the world's largest trade deficits. Yet in none of the countries named above, including the Unites States and UK, has manufacturing job loss been associated with declines in absolute levels of manufacturing output. On the contrary, the volume of manufacturing production, as measured by real value added, more than doubled in the United States, France, Germany, Japan, and Italy between 1970 and 2017. Even the UK, whose manufacturing sector fared worst of all among this group, saw a 25 percent increase in manufacturing real value added over this period. To be sure, low- and middle-income countries are producing more and more goods for export to high-income countries; however, deindustrialization in the latter cannot simply be the result of productive capacity moving to the former, since the high-income countries produced more manufactured goods at the end of the 2010s than they had anytime in the past. In line with automation theorists' core expectations, more goods are being produced but by fewer workers.

It is on this basis that commentators typically cite rapidly rising labor productivity, rather than an influx of low-cost imports from abroad, as the primary cause of industrial job loss in advanced economies.[10] On closer inspection, however, this explanation also turns out to be inadequate. Manufacturing productivity has been growing at a sluggish pace for decades, leading economist Robert Solow to quip, "We see the computer age everywhere, except in the productivity statistics."[11] Automation theorists discuss this "productivity paradox" as a problem for their account—explaining it in terms of weak demand for products, or the persistent availability of low-wage workers—but they understate its true significance. This is partly due to the appearance of steady labor-productivity growth in US manufacturing, at an average rate of around 3 percent per year since 1950. On that basis, Erik Brynjolfsson and Andrew McAfee suggest, automation could show up in the compounding effects of exponential growth, rather than an uptick in the growth rate.[12]

However, official US manufacturing growth-rate statistics are vastly overinflated, since they log the production of computers with higher processing speeds as equivalent to the production of more computers.[13] For that reason, government statistics suggest that productivity levels in the computers and electronics subsector rose at a galloping average annual rate of over 10 percent per year between 1987 and 2011, even as productivity growth rates outside of that subsector fell to around 2 percent per year over the same period.[14] Starting in 2011, trends across the manufacturing sector worsened: real output per person employed in the sector as a whole was lower in 2017 than in 2010. Productivity growth rates in manufacturing collapsed precisely when, according to automation theorists, they were supposed to be rising rapidly due to advancing technologies.

Correction of US manufacturing-productivity statistics brings them more into line with trends in countries like Germany and Japan, where manufacturing-productivity growth rates have fallen dramatically since their postwar peaks. In Germany, manufacturing productivity grew at an average annual rate of 6.3 percent per year in the 1950s and '60s, falling to 2.4 percent from 2000 to 2017. This downward trend was to some extent an expected result of the end of an era of rapid catch-up growth. However, it should still be surprising to the automation theorists, since Germany and Japan have raced ahead of the United States in the field of industrial robotics. Indeed, the robots used in Tesla's largely automated car factory in California were made by a German robotics company.[15] As of 2016, German and Japanese firms deployed about 60 percent more industrial robots per manufacturing worker, compared to the US.[16]

Yet deindustrialization has continued to take place in all these countries, despite lackluster manufacturing-productivity growth rates; that is, it has taken place as the automation theorists expect, but not for the reasons they offer. To explore the causes of deindustrialization in more detail, I rely on the following definitions. *Output*, as used both above and below, is a measure of the volume of production (how much is produced), in terms of real or inflation-adjusted "value added" in a given economic sector.[17] Gross domestic product, or

GDP, is just value added for the economy as a whole. *Employment*, as I use it here, is a measure of the number of workers rather than of hours worked—the latter are typically unavailable outside of wealthier countries—while *productivity* is the ratio of output to employment: the more output is produced per worker, the higher that worker's productivity level. For any economic sector, the rate of growth of output (ΔO) minus the rate of growth of labor productivity (ΔP) equals the rate of growth of employment (ΔE). Thus, $\Delta O - \Delta P = \Delta E$.[18] This equation is true by definition. If the output of automobiles grows by 3 percent per year, and productivity in the automotive industry grows by 2 percent per year, then employment in that industry must have risen by one percent per year $(3 - 2 = 1)$. Contrariwise, if output grows by 3 percent per year and productivity grows by 4 percent per year, employment will have contracted by 1 percent per year $(3 - 4 = -1)$.

Disaggregation of manufacturing-output growth rates in France provides us with a sense of the typical pattern playing out across the high-income countries (Figure 2.1).[19] During the so-called golden age of postwar capitalism, productivity growth rates in French manufacturing were much higher than they are today—5.2 percent per year, on average, between 1950 and 1973—but output growth rates were even higher than that—5.9 percent per year. As a result, employment had to have grown steadily, at a pace of 0.7 percent per year. Since 1973, both output and productivity growth rates have declined, but output growth rates fell much more sharply than productivity growth rates. By the early years of the twenty-first century, productivity was rising at a much less rapid pace than it had during the postwar era, at 2.7 percent per year. However, slower productivity growth rates were now faster than their corresponding industrial output growth rates, at 0.9 percent. The result was that manufacturing employment contracted rapidly, by 1.7 percent per year. Even before that contraction got going, deindustrialization had already technically begun: as soon as the rate of growth of manufacturing employment consistently fell below the rate of growth of the total workforce, the manufacturing employment share started its downward trend.

Figure 2.1. French Manufacturing Sector, 1950–2017

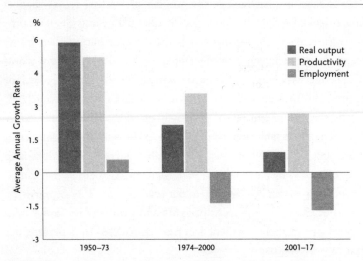

Source: Conference Board, International Comparisons of Productivity and Unit Labour Costs, July 2018 edition.

This disaggregation helps explain why automation theorists falsely perceive productivity to be growing at a rapid pace in manufacturing. Productivity growth rates have been high relative to output growth rates, but not because productivity has been growing more rapidly than before—which would be a sure sign of accelerating automation. On the contrary, the key to this trend is that output has been growing much more slowly than before. The same pattern can be seen in the statistics of other countries: no absolute decline in levels of manufacturing production took place—more and more was produced—but the rate at which output grows declined, so output growth came to be consistently slower than productivity growth (Table 2.1). As industrial output growth rates fell below corresponding productivity growth rates in country after country, quantitative declines in economic indicators became qualitative in their effects: manufacturing employment shares fell progressively. Worsening economic stagnation thus combined with a limited technological dynamism to generate labor's global deindustrialization.

Table 2.1. Manufacturing Growth Rates, 1950–2017

		Output	Productivity	Employment
USA	1950–73	4.4%	3.1%	1.2%
	1974–2000	3.1%	3.3%	-0.2%
	2001–17	1.2%	3.2%	-1.8%
Germany	1950–73	7.6%	5.7%	1.8%
	1974–2000	1.3%	2.5%	-1.1%
	2001–17	2.0%	2.2%	-0.2%
Japan	1950–73	14.9%	10.1%	4.3%
	1974–2000	2.8%	3.4%	-0.6%
	2001–17	1.7%	2.7%	-1.1%

Source: Conference Board, International Comparisons of Productivity and Unit Labour Costs, July 2018 edition.

Such "output-led" deindustrialization is impossible to explain in purely technological terms.[20] In their search for alternative perspectives, economists have mostly preferred to describe this trend as a harmless evolutionary feature of advanced economies.[21] However, that perspective is itself at a loss to explain extreme variations in the GDP per capita levels at which this supposedly evolutionary economic shift has taken place. Deindustrialization unfolded first in high-income countries in the late 1960s and early 1970s, at the tail end of a period in which levels of income per person had converged across the United States, Europe, and Japan. In the decades that followed, deindustrialization then spread "prematurely" to middle- and low-income countries, with larger variations in incomes per capita (Figure 2.2).[22] In the late 1970s, deindustrialization arrived in southern Europe; much of Latin America, parts of East and Southeast Asia, and southern Africa followed in the 1980s and '90s. Peak industrialization levels in many poorer countries were so low that it may be more accurate to say that they never industrialized in the first place.[23]

Figure 2.2. Global Waves of Deindustrialization, 1950–2010

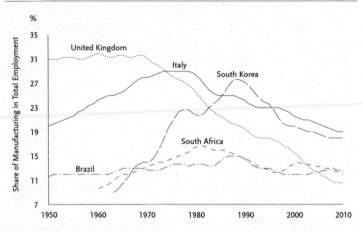

Source: Groningen Growth and Development Centre, 10-Sector Database, January 2015 edition.

By the end of the twentieth century, it was possible to speak of a global wave of deindustrialization: worldwide manufacturing employment rose in absolute terms by 0.4 percent per year between 1991 and 2016, but that was much slower than the overall growth of the global labor force, with the result that the manufacturing share of total employment declined by 3 percentage points over the same period.[24] China is a key exception, but only a partial one (Figure 2.3). In the mid 1990s, Chinese state-owned enterprises shed millions of workers, sending manufacturing-employment shares on a steady downward trajectory.[25] China reindustrialized, in employment terms, starting in the early 2000s, but then it began to deindustrialize once again in the mid 2010s. Its manufacturing-employment share has since dropped significantly, from 19.3 percent in 2013 to 17.2 percent in 2018. If deindustrialization cannot be explained by either automation or the internal evolution of advanced economies, what could be its source?

Blight of Manufacturing Overcapacity

What the economists' accounts fail to register in their explanations of deindustrialization is also what is missing from the automation

Figure 2.3. Deindustrialization in China, India and Mexico, 1980–2017

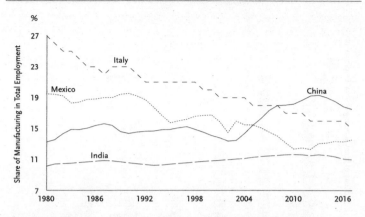

Source: Conference Board, International Comparisons of Productivity and Unit Labour Costs, July 2018 edition.

theorists' accounts. The truth is that rates of output growth in manufacturing have tended to decline, not only in this or that country, but *worldwide* (Figure 2.4).[26] In the 1950s and '60s, global-manufacturing production expanded at an average annual rate of 7.1 percent per year, in real terms. That rate fell progressively to 4.8 percent in the 1970s and to 3.0 percent between 1980 and 2007. From the 2008 crisis up to 2014, manufacturing output expanded at just 1.6 percent per year, on a world scale—that is, at less than a quarter of the pace achieved during the postwar "golden age."[27] It is worth noting that these figures include the dramatic expansion of manufacturing productive capacity in China.

Again, it is the incredible degree of slowdown in the rate at which manufacturing production expands, visible on the world scale, that explains why manufacturing-productivity growth appears to have advanced at a rapid clip, even though it was actually much slower than in previous eras. More and more *is* produced with fewer workers, as the automation theorists claim, but not because technological change has given rise to high rates of productivity growth. Far from it—productivity growth in manufacturing has appeared rapid only because the yardstick of output growth, against which it is measured, has been shrinking.

Figure 2.4. World Manufacturing and Agricultural Production, 1950–2014

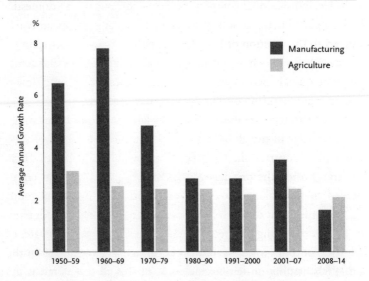

Source: World Trade Organization, International Trade Statistics 2015, Table A1a, World Merchandise Exports, Production and GDP, 1950–2014.

Following economist Robert Brenner, I argue that global waves of deindustrialization find their origins not in runaway technical change, but first and foremost in a worsening overcapacity in world markets for manufactured goods.[28] The rise in overcapacity developed stepwise after World War II. In the immediate postwar period, the United States hosted the most dynamic economy in the world, with the most advanced technologies: in 1950, output per hour worked in the US economy was more than twice as high as output per hour in European countries.[29] Under the threat of Communist expansion within Europe, as well as in East and Southeast Asia, the US proved willing to share its technological largesse with its former imperial competitors Germany and Japan, as well as with other "frontline" countries, in order to bring them all under the US security umbrella.[30] In the first few decades of the post–World War II era, these technology transfers were a major boost to economic growth in European countries and Japan, opening up opportunities for rapid export-led expansion. This strategy was supported by the devaluation of their currencies against the dollar in 1949, which improved these countries' international competitiveness at the expense of domestic, working-class buying power (a move that in many European countries led to the eviction of left political parties from government).[31] However, as Brenner has argued, rising manufacturing capacity across the globe quickly generated overcapacity, issuing in a "long downturn" in manufacturing-output growth rates.

What mattered here was not only the later build-out of manufacturing capacity in the global South, but the earlier creation of such capacity in countries like Germany, France, Italy, and Japan. These countries hosted the first low-cost producers in the postwar era to succeed, first, in taking shares in global markets for industrial goods and, second, in invading the previously impenetrable US domestic market. Due to rising competition with lower-cost producers, rates of industrial output growth in the US began to decline starting in the late 1960s, issuing in deindustrialization in employment terms. As the US responded to heightened import penetration in the early 1970s by breaking up the Bretton Woods order and devaluing the dollar—which increased US firms' international competitiveness—these same problems spread from North America and northwestern Europe to the rest of the European continent and Japan.[32]

Intensifying competition among firms in these high-income regions did not dissuade more countries from building up manufacturing capacity, adopting export-led growth strategies, and entering global markets for manufactured goods. As additional manufacturing capacity appeared and entered the fray of international competition, falling rates of manufacturing-output growth and consequent labor deindustrialization spread to more regions: Latin America, the Middle East, Asia, and Africa, as well as to the global economy taken as a whole. Deindustrialization came to most global South regions in the aftermath of the 1982 Third World debt crisis, amid the imposition of IMF-led structural adjustment programs. As trade liberalization opened the borders of poorer countries to imports, while financial liberalization brought hot money flowing into "emerging markets," their currencies revalued sharply. Unit labor costs in these regions rose just as markets were becoming more overcrowded, with the result that firms found themselves able neither to compete with imports nor to export their wares abroad.[33]

Deindustrialization was a matter not only of technological advance, but also of global redundancy of productive and technological capacities. In more crowded international markets, rapid rates of industrial expansion became more difficult to achieve.[34] The mechanism transmitting this problem across the world was depressed prices in global markets for manufactured goods (which also explains why shifting currency valuations played such a major role in determining competitiveness).[35] As Harvard economist Dani Rodrik notes, "Developing countries 'imported' deindustrialization from the advanced countries" because they were "exposed to the relative price trends" coming from the capitalist core.[36]

Everywhere, depressed prices for manufactures led to falling income-per-unit capital ratios (falling capital productivity), then to falling rates of profit, then to lower rates of investment, and finally to lower output growth rates.[37] In this environment, firms faced heightened competition for market share: as overall growth rates slowed, the only way for new firms to grow quickly was to steal market shares from established firms. The latter responded by retreating to the apex of global value chains. Overcapacity explains why, from the early 1970s, productivity growth rates fell less severely than output growth rates. Firms either raised their productivity levels as best they could— in an effort to keep up with their competitors despite the slower growth of the demand for their products—or else went under, disappearing from statistical averages.[38] The implementation of technological innovations, although occurring at a slower pace than before, generated sector-wide job loss.[39] As output growth rates fell toward (and in many cases below) productivity growth rates, in one country after another, deindustrialization spread worldwide.

Explaining global waves of deindustrialization in terms of global overcapacity rather than industrial automation allows us to understand a number of features of this phenomenon that otherwise appear paradoxical. For example, rising overcapacity explains why deindustrialization has been accompanied not only by ongoing efforts to develop new labor-saving technologies, but also by the build-out of gigantic, labor-intensive supply chains—usually with a more damaging environmental impact.[40] A key turning point in that story came in the 1960s, when low-cost Japanese and German products invaded the US domestic market, sending the US industrial import penetration ratio soaring from less than 7 percent in the mid '60s to 16 percent in the early '70s.[41] From that point forward, it became clear that high levels of labor productivity would no longer serve as a shield against competition from lower-wage countries. The firms that did best in this context were the ones that responded by globalizing production. Facing competition on prices, US multinational corporations (MNCs) built international supply chains, shifting the more labor-intensive components of their production processes abroad and playing suppliers against one another to achieve the best prices.[42] In the mid '60s the first export-processing zones opened in Taiwan and South Korea. Even Silicon Valley, which formerly produced its computer chips locally in the San Jose area, shifted its production to low-wage areas, using lower grades of technology while benefiting from laxer laws around pollution and workers' safety.[43] MNCs in Germany and Japan adopted similar strategies, which were everywhere supported by new transportation and communication infrastructures.[44]

The globalization of production allowed the world's wealthiest economies to retain manufacturing capacity, but it did not reverse the overall trend toward labor deindustrialization. As supply chains were built out across the world, firms in more and more countries were pulled into the swirl of world market competition. In some countries, this move was accompanied by shifts in the location of new plants: rust belts, oriented toward production for domestic markets, went into decline; sun belts, integrated into global supply networks, expanded dramatically. Chattanooga grew at the expense of Detroit, Juárez at the expense of Mexico City, Guangdong at the expense of Dongbei.[45] Yet given the overall slowdown in rates of world market expansion, this reorientation toward the world market resulted in lackluster outcomes: the rise of sun belts failed to balance out the decline of rust belts, resulting in global deindustrialization.

At the same time, global manufacturing overcapacity explains why the countries that have succeeded in attaining a high degree of robotization are not those that have seen the worst degree of deindustrialization. Measured in terms of robots deployed per thousand workers in manufacturing, South Korea (63), Germany (31), and Japan (30) had advanced much further along the road to full automation, as compared to the United States (19) and UK (7), in 2016. Yet manufacturing employment shares in that same year were significantly higher in South Korea (17 percent), Germany (17 percent), and Japan (15 percent) than in the US (8 percent) and UK (8 percent). In the context of intense global competition, high degrees of robotization translate into international competitive advantages, helping firms win larger shares of world markets for the goods they produce. Unlike workers in the United States, workers in European and East Asian firms believe that automation helps preserve their jobs.[46] Chinese firms have also been major players in global markets for manufactured goods, providing China's industrial sector with a gigantic boost in terms of both output growth and employment growth, yet Chinese firms advanced on this front not due to high levels of robotization—in 2016, China deployed just 7 robots per thousand workers in manufacturing—but rather due to a mix of low wages, moderate to advanced technologies, and strong infrastructural capacities. Still, the result was the same: in spite of system-wide overcapacity and slow growth rates, China has industrialized rapidly because its firms have been able to take market share away from other firms—not only in the United States, but also in countries like Mexico and Brazil. It could not have been otherwise. In an environment where average growth rates are low, firms can only achieve high rates of growth by taking market share from their competitors. Whether China will be able to retain its competitive position as its wage levels rise remains an open question; Chinese firms have been robotizing to try to head off this possibility.[47]

CHAPTER 3

In the Shadow of Stagnation

THE EVIDENCE I CITED in the previous chapter to explain job loss in the manufacturing sector through worsening overcapacity may appear to have little purchase on the larger, economy-wide trends that automation theorists attribute to growing technological dynamism: stagnant wages, falling labor shares of income, declining labor force participation rates, and jobless recoveries after recessions. Automation may therefore still seem a good explanation for the decline in the demand for labor across the service sectors of each country's economy, and so across the world economy as a whole. Yet automation has had even less of an impact in services than it has in manufacturing. In fact, the broader problem of declining labor demand also turns out to be better explained by the worsening industrial stagnation I have described than it is by widespread technological dynamism. This is because, as rates of manufacturing-output growth stagnated in one country after another from the 1970s onward, no other sector appeared on the scene to replace industry as a major economic-growth engine. Instead, the slowdown in manufacturing-output growth rates was accompanied by a slowdown in overall GDP growth rates.

Running Down the Growth Engine

These entwined trends are easily visible in the economic statistics of high-income countries. France is a striking example (Figure 3.1). In France, real manufacturing value added (MVA) rose at 5.9 percent per year between 1950 and 1973, while real value added in the total economy (GDP) rose at 5.1 percent per year.[1] From 1973 on, both growth measures declined significantly: by the 2001–17 period, MVA was rising at only 0.9 percent per year, while GDP was rising at a faster, but still sluggish, pace of 1.2 percent per year. Note that during the 1950s and '60s, MVA growth generally led the economy. Manufacturing served as the major engine of overall growth. Beginning in 1973, MVA growth rates trailed overall economic growth. Similar patterns can be seen in other countries (Table 3.1). Export-led growth engines sputtered; as they did so, overall rates of economic growth slowed to a crawl in country after country.[2]

Economists studying deindustrialization often point out that while manufacturing has declined as a share of nominal GDP, it has maintained, until recently, a more or less steady share of real GDP,

Figure 3.1. French Manufacturing and Total Output Growth, 1950–2017

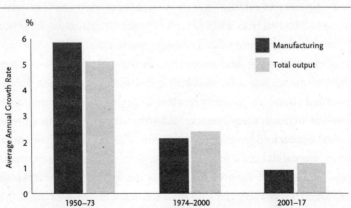

Source: Conference Board, International Comparisons of Productivity and Unit Labour Costs, July 2018 edition.

Table 3.1. Manufacturing and GDP Growth Rates, 1950–2017

		MVA	GDP
USA	1950–73	4.4%	4.0%
	1974–2000	3.1%	3.2%
	2001–17	1.2%	1.9%
Germany	1950–73	7.6%	5.7%
	1974–2000	1.3%	1.9%
	2001–17	2.0%	1.4%
Japan	1950–73	14.9%	9.3%
	1974–2000	2.8%	3.2%
	2001–17	1.7%	1.9%

Source: Conference Board, International Comparisons of Productivity and Unit Labour Costs,
July 2018 edition.

which is to say that between 1973 and 2000, real MVA grew at approximately the same pace as real GDP.[3] There was no significant shift in demand from industry to services. What that meant in practice was that, as manufacturing became less dynamic, so did the overall economy.

The primary mechanism transmitting the downturn from manufacturing to the wider economy was a slowing pace of investment, corresponding to a decline in the demand for goods and services used to expand production. That, in turn, depressed consumption demand through reduced hiring. Seen from the perspective of the total economy, overcapacity appears as underinvestment—albeit one without a clear solution, since it is structural in character. Across the advanced capitalist countries, the growth rate of the capital stock (that is, the value of structures, equipment, and software measured in constant prices) has declined over time (Table 3.2). For example, in the United States, the capital stock grew at a rate of 3.6 percent per year between 1951 and 1973, falling to 2.8 percent per year between 1974 and 2000, and 1.8 percent per year between 2001 and 2017 (after 2009, the capital stock grew at an average annual pace of just 1.3 percent).[4] As the average firm has invested less in expanding its fixed capital base, average labor productivity growth rates have declined, as well. That is because labor-saving innovations tend to be embodied in capital goods, or else typically require complementary investments in capital goods to be realized.[5] In the United States, labor productivity grew at a rate of 2.4 percent per year between 1951 and 1973, falling to 1.4 percent per year between 1974 and 2000, and 1.2 percent per year between 2001 and 2017 (between 2011 and 2017, productivity grew at just 0.7 percent per year). Similar trends unfolded in other high-income countries and were even more severe.

Table 3.2. Capital Stock and Labor Productivity Growth Rates, 1950–2017

		Capital Stock	Productivity
USA	1950–73	3.6%	2.4%
	1974–2000	2.8%	1.4%
	2001–17	1.8%	1.2%
Germany	1950–73	6.9%	4.7%
	1974–2000	2.3%	1.7%
	2001–17	1.0%	0.7%
Japan	1950–73	9.3%	7.6%
	1974–2000	4.7%	2.5%
	2001–17	0.7%	0.7%

Source: Conference Board, Total Economy Database, April 2019 edition, and Groningen Growth and Development Centre, Penn World Table 9.1, September 2019 edition, retrieved from FRED, Federal Reserve Bank of St. Louis.

The tendency to economy-wide stagnation, associated with the decline in manufacturing dynamism, then explains the system-wide decline in the demand for labor, and so also the problems that the automation theorists cite: stagnant real wages, falling labor shares of income, and so on.[6] The economy-wide pattern of declining labor demand has not been the result of rising productivity growth rates, associated with automation in the service sector. On the contrary, productivity has grown even more slowly outside of the manufacturing sector than inside of it. In Germany and Japan, for example, while productivity in the manufacturing sector was rising at an average annual rate of 2.2 and 2.7 percent, respectively between 2001 and 2017, productivity in the economy as a whole was rising at just 0.7 percent in both countries. Once again, the mistake of the automation theorists is to assume that productivity is rising at a rapid pace; whereas in fact, output growth rates have declined sharply over time.

These trends are as visible in the world economy—including China—as they are in the high-income countries (Figure 3.2). In the 1950s and '60s, global MVA growth and GDP growth were expanding at rapid clips of 7.1 and 5.0 percent respectively, with MVA growth leading GDP growth by a significant margin. From the 1970s onward, as global MVA growth slowed, so did global GDP growth. In most of the decades that followed, global MVA growth continued to lead GDP growth, but by a much smaller margin. Between 2008 and 2014, both rates grew at the exceptionally slow pace of 1.6 percent per year. Again, the implication is that as manufacturing growth rates declined, nothing emerged to replace industry as a

Figure 3.2. World Manufacturing and Total Production, 1950–2014

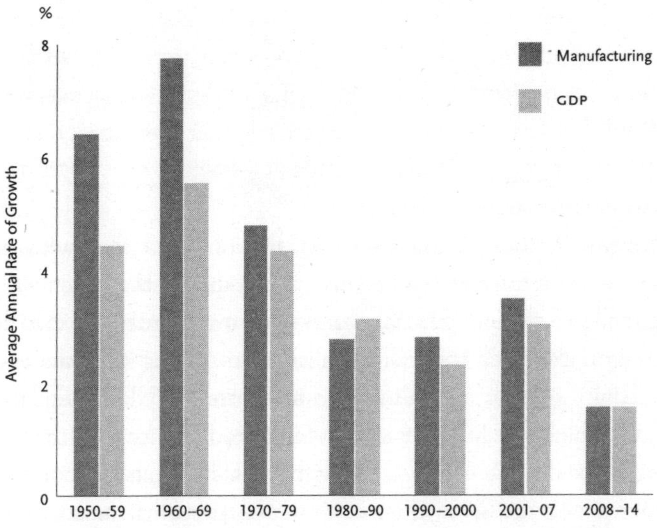

Source: World Trade Organization, International Trade Statistics 2015, Table A1a, World Merchandise Exports, Production and GDP, 1950–2014.

growth engine. Not all regions of the world economy experienced this slowdown in the same way or to the same extent, but even countries like China that have grown quickly had to contend with this global slowdown and its consequences. After 2010, China's economic growth rate slowed considerably, and its economy has been deindustrializing. The same is true in India. Other BRICS economies— South Africa, Russia, and Brazil—fared even worse: by 2011, their growth rates were collapsing, and that was before the COVID-19 crisis, which has resulted in significant cuts to manufacturing production worldwide. Global MVA and GDP growth rates are likely to decline further in the 2020s.

Reflection on more than half a century of economic trends demonstrates that manufacturing was a unique engine of economic growth.[7] Industrial production tends to be amenable to incremental increases in productivity, achieved via technologies that can be repurposed across numerous lines. Industry also benefits from major economies of scale, which raise productivity levels as the volume of production increases. In fact, according to an economic regularity known as Verdoorn's law, the faster the rate of growth of industrial output, the faster too is the rate of productivity growth. Some commentators describe the present period of economic stagnation in terms of an exhaustion of the frontiers of technological advance—as if there were nothing left to invent—but it is more likely that low rates of industrial productivity growth are the result of a slower pace of industrial expansion rather than the reverse.[8]

Meanwhile, there is no necessary boundary to the industrial sector: industry consists of all economic activities that are capable of being rendered via an industrial process, and more and more activities are so rendered over time. The reallocation of workers from low-productivity jobs in agriculture, domestic industry, and domestic services to high-productivity jobs in factories raises levels of income per worker and hence economic growth rates. The countries that have caught up with the West in terms of income—such as Japan, South Korea, and Taiwan—mostly did so by industrializing. They exploited opportunities to produce for the world market, at increasing scale and with advanced technologies, allowing them to grow at speeds that would have been unachievable had they depended on domestic market demand alone.[9]

Manufacturing's importance may seem surprising given that, in terms of value added, the sector accounts for a shrinking share of economic activity. However, in terms of gross output—which unlike value added includes the costs of intermediate inputs (that is, the goods and services consumed by firms)—manufacturing's "footprint" on the wider economy is significantly larger.[10] Even in the United States, a country with a large trade deficit, manufacturing gross output accounted for 42 percent of total GDP in 2000. That share fell to 30 percent over the course of the 2010s (a decade that saw worsening economic stagnation). In Japan, manufacturing gross output's share of GDP was still higher: 59 percent in 2017.[11]

The Lack of Alternatives

When the growth engine of industrialization has sputtered due to the replication of technical capacities, international redundancy, and fierce competition for markets, there has been no replacement for it as a source of rapid growth. Instead of a reallocation of workers from low-productivity jobs to high-productivity ones, the reverse takes place. Workers pool in low-productivity jobs, mostly in the service sector. As countries have deindustrialized, they have also seen a massive buildup of financialized capital, chasing returns to the ownership of relatively liquid assets rather than investing long-term in new fixed capital.[12] In spite of the high degree of overcapacity in industry, there is nowhere more profitable in the real economy for capital to invest itself. If there had been, we would have evidence of it in higher rates of capital accumulation and hence higher GDP growth rates. Instead, what we see is ongoing disinvestment—with corporations using idle cash to buy back their own shares or pay out dividends—and falling long-term interest rates, as the supply of loanable funds far outstrips demand.

Under these conditions, huge quantities of money have flowed into financial assets. The expansion of gigantic asset bubbles periodically creates a "wealth effect" as richer households use more of their annual incomes for consumption, since their assets appear to be saving money for them.[13] The US economy has become ever more dependent on such bubble-driven spending.[14] When the bubbles pop, those same wealthy households withdraw from consumption to pay down their debts, generating long periods of economic malaise— sometimes called "Japanification," since the first country to experience balance-sheet stagnation was Japan, after its bubble popped in 1991.[15] Following the deflation of economic bubbles, the onset of slower growth renders manifest the absence of a sustainable, alternative growth engine to manufacturing. Indeed, in spite of their financialization, the fortunes of wealthier economies have remained strongly tied to the fate of their manufacturing sectors (which helps explain why firms have reacted to overaccumulation by trying to make their existing manufacturing capacity more flexible and efficient, rather than ceding ground to lower-cost firms from other countries).[16]

For example, in the late 1980s and early '90s, US manufacturing briefly recovered from its malaise due to a dramatic decline in the value of the dollar, which—when combined with stagnant real wages and falling corporate taxes—improved the international competitiveness of American industrial firms significantly at the expense of the US domestic working class.[17] This period saw a revival in the fortunes of the US economy and has been studied as a mini-boom led by information and communications technology (ICT). But the US economy in this period did not function in isolation of global trends. The decline in the value of the dollar after 1985 corresponded to a rise in the value of European and Japanese currencies, issuing in declining manufacturing competitiveness for European and Japanese firms, falling rates of fixed capital investment, and slowing economic growth rates.[18] There was no ICT-related economic upturn in these regions. On the contrary, rates of economic growth slowed secularly across Europe and Japan from the 1970s to the early 2000s. In Japan, capital exiting from manufacturing flowed into financial assets, leading to the expansion of its infamous real estate bubble—the largest of the asset-bubble era—whose later deflation sent the Japanese economy into a tailspin and threatened to take down the world economy. Emergency response measures employed by the Bank of Japan in the early 1990s later provided the template on which both the US Federal Reserve and the European Central Bank relied in the aftermath of the 2008 financial crash.[19]

A wider global crisis was averted in the mid 1990s only because the United States proved willing to engineer a revaluation of the dollar that gave the Japanese and German economies room to recover their international positions to some extent. However, an unintended consequence of this rescue operation was that the United States and the East Asian countries whose currencies had been tied to the dollar, such as South Korea, then saw their nascent booms transformed into bubbles. Their manufacturing sectors no longer served as engines of a more expansive economic growth, and capital fled into financial assets. The deflation of the resulting asset bubbles—in East Asia in 1997, and in the US in 2001 and again in 2007—revealed deeper structural tendencies toward stagnation due to industrial overcapacity and underinvestment.[20]

The failure to find a sustainable alternative to the manufacturing growth engine also explains why governments in poorer countries have encouraged domestic producers to try to break into international markets for manufactures, even though they are oversupplied.[21] Nothing has replaced those markets as a major source of globally accessible demand. Overcapacity exists in agriculture, too, and is even worse there than in industry; meanwhile services, which are mostly non-tradable, make up only a tiny share of global exports.[22] If countries are to retain any dependable link to the international market under these conditions, they must find some way to insert themselves into industrial lines. Between 2001 and 2007, rising rates of global manufacturing expansion briefly created an opening for export-led development across the BRICS economies (Brazil, Russia, India, China, and South Africa), inspiring some economists to theorize that the incomes of richer and poorer regions were converging, reversing their centuries-long divergence due to the lasting legacy of colonialism.[23] However, this mini-boom turned out to depend on debt-fueled consumption in the high-income countries, which ended abruptly after the 2007 deflation of the US housing bubble—once again revealing a wider tendency to industrial overcapacity and underinvestment worldwide.

Economic downshifts were particularly devastating for low- and middle-income countries in this era, not only because they were poorer, but also because those downshifts took place in an era of rapid labor force expansion. From 1980 to 2018, the world's workforce, both waged and unwaged, grew by about 75 percent, adding more than 1.5 billion people to the world's labor markets.[24] These labor market entrants, living mostly in poorer countries, had the misfortune of growing up and looking for work at a time when global industrial overcapacity began to shape patterns of economic growth in postcolonial countries. Declining rates of manufactured import growth in the United States and Europe in the late 1970s and early '80s ignited the 1982 Third World debt crisis, followed by IMF-led structural adjustment, which pushed countries to deepen their imbrications in global markets at a time of ever-slower global growth and rising competition from China.[25]

Some may respond that such low rates of global growth are in fact nothing out of the ordinary, if only we shift our baseline from the exceptional postwar "golden age" to previous periods, such as the pre–World War I era. But a global perspective on the decline in the demand for labor provides the answer to this objection. It is true that during the Belle Epoque (1870–1913), average rates of economic growth were more comparable to growth rates today.[26] However, in that period, large sections of the population still lived in the countryside and produced much of what they needed to live.[27] European empires overran the globe, not only limiting the diffusion of new manufacturing technologies to a few regions, but also actively deindustrializing the rest of the world economy.[28] Yet in spite of the much more limited sphere in which labor markets were active—and in which industrialization took place—the pre–World War I era, like the interwar period, was marked by a persistently low demand for labor, making for employment insecurity, rising inequality, and tumultuous social movements aimed at transforming economic relations.[29] In this respect, the world of today *does* look like the world of the Belle Epoque.[30] The difference, however, is that today a much larger share of the world's population depends on finding work in labor markets to live, and thus finds itself subject to the insecurity attendant on looking for work in a low-labor-demand economy. Meanwhile, average economic growth rates in our times are likely to fall further as unresolved tendencies to economic stagnation are compounded by COVID-19. Historical precedents suggest that, in contrast to wars, pandemics are followed by long-lasting declines in GDP growth rates, rather than post-pandemic economic booms.[31]

Technology's Role

What automation theorists describe as the result of rising technological dynamism is actually the consequence of worsening economic stagnation, following on decades of manufacturing overcapacity and underinvestment. These theorists assume that an accelerating pace of productivity growth is the main driver of the declining demand for labor, when, in reality, the main driver is a decelerating pace of output growth. This mistake is not without reason. The demand for labor is determined by the gap between productivity and output growth rates. Reading the shrinkage of this gap the wrong way around—that is, as due to rising productivity rather than falling output rates—is what generates the upside-down world of the automation discourse. Proponents of this discourse then search for the technological evidence that supports their view of the causes of low labor demand. In making this leap, the automation theorists miss the true story that explains this phenomenon: overcrowded global markets for manufactures, declining rates of investment in fixed capital, and a corresponding economic slowdown.

Yet even if automation is not itself the primary cause of a low demand for labor, it is still true that in a slow-growing economy, technological change can give rise to massive job destruction: witness, for example, the US manufacturing sector's rapid job shedding between 2000–2010. Were the economy growing quickly, new jobs would easily be generated to replace those that had been lost (what we would be seeing, then, would be a classic example of "creative destruction").[32] By contrast, in an environment of persistent economic slowdown, workers who lose their jobs face significant hurdles in looking for work. A clarification of these wider economic conditions allows us to revisit the question of technology's role in job loss and explain why "automation" may be a misleading term for how it typically occurs.

In seeking to understand the links between technology and job loss, the automation theorists do themselves a disservice. Across much of the literature, research and development in the digital age is presented as a matter of engineers in white lab coats following the technology "wherever it leads them" without having to worry about "end results" or "social outcomes."[33] Graphs of exponentially rising computing capacities—with Moore's law of rising processor speeds standing in for technical change in general—suggest that technology develops automatically down pre-set paths.[34] That suggestion in turn feeds into the fantasy of a coming "singularity," when machine intelligence will finally give birth to science fiction–style artificial general intelligence, developing at speeds far beyond human comprehension.[35]

In reality, technological development is highly resource intensive, forcing researchers to pursue certain paths of inquiry at the expense of others. In our society, firms must focus on developing technologies that lead to profitable outcomes. Turning profits off of digital services, which are mostly offered to end users for free online, has proven elusive. Rather than focus on generating advances in artificial general intelligence, engineers at Facebook spend their time studying slot machines to figure out how to get people addicted to their website, so that they keep coming back to check for notifications, post content, and view advertisements.[36] The result is that, like all modern technologies, these digital offerings are far from "socially neutral."[37] The internet, as developed by the US government and shaped by capitalist enterprises, is not the only internet that could exist.[38] The same can be

said of robotics: in choosing among possible pathways of technological progress, capital's command over the work process remains para-
mount.[39] Technologies that would empower line workers are not
pursued, whereas technologies allowing for detailed surveillance of
those same workers are fast becoming hot commodities.[40] These
features of technological change in capitalist societies have important
implications for anyone seeking to turn existing technical means
toward new, emancipatory aims. Profit-driven technological advances
are highly unlikely to overcome human drudgery as such, at least on
their own, especially where labor remains cheap, plentiful, and easily
exploited.

Nevertheless, even if technical change will not end work altogether, it does periodically result in sweeping job destruction in
certain industries. Sometimes that's because technologies allow for
the full automation of a particular work process. More often, it is
because technical innovations allow firms to overcome long-standing
impediments to raising labor productivity in specific industries.
Agriculture, for example, was one of the first sectors to be transformed by modern production methods: in the fifteenth- and
sixteenth-century English countryside, new forms of animal
husbandry on enclosed farms were combined with crop rotation to
raise yields. Yet farming remained difficult to mechanize, due to the
uneven terrain of fields and seasonal cycles, and for centuries it
continued to be a major source of employment.[41] In the 1940s,
advances in synthetic fertilizers, the hybridization of crops, the mechanization of farming implements, and the development of pesticides
finally made it possible to develop industrialized forms of agricultural
production and animal husbandry, causing operative logics to shift.[42]

Labor productivity took off, as farms came to resemble open-air
factories. Given the limits to the growth of the demand for agricultural outputs, the sector then shed workers at an incredible pace. As
late as 1950, agriculture employed 24 percent of the workforce in
West Germany, 25 percent in France, 42 percent in Japan, and 47
percent in Italy; by 2010, all of these shares were under 5 percent.
During the 1950s and '60s Green Revolution, methods of

industrialized agriculture were adapted for tropical climates, with stunning consequences for global agricultural employment: in the 1980s, the majority of the world's workers were still in agriculture; by 2018 that figure had fallen to 28 percent.[43] Thus, the major destroyer of livelihoods in the twentieth century was not "silicon capitalism" but nitrogen capitalism. No automatic mechanism existed within the labor market to ensure that new jobs were created for the hundreds of millions of people who were forced to exit from agriculture.

In the twenty-first century, as in previous periods, inventors and engineers will figure out how to overcome resistances to industrial development in additional lines of production. The problem is that, in an era of slower economic growth, productivity growth rates tend to fall. Firms forgo major investments in expanding their productive capacities; many new gadgets on display in trade shows thus fail to find their way onto shop floors. This is not to say that productivity will not grow at a fast pace in some industries. For example, long-haul trucking, retail, and wholesale trade may shed jobs in the coming years due to a variety of technological breakthroughs.[44] However, it is hard to say what share of these jobs will be eliminated, as rates of capital accumulation and labor-productivity growth decelerate across the economy.

On the global scale, much more concerning than the mechanization of trucks or warehouses would be the mechanization of apparel and footwear industries and of electronics assembly. These sectors employ large numbers of people worldwide and generate foreign exchange for otherwise cash-strapped economies.[45] Sewing in particular has long been resistant to technological modernization: it involves detailed work with fabrics, which machines have trouble manipulating; the last major innovation in the field was the Singer sewing machine in the 1850s. Electronics assembly work, although of more recent vintage, has proven similarly resistant to labor-saving innovation, since it too requires the delicate manipulation of tiny parts. As technological laggards within larger, highly mechanized production processes, these jobs were some of the first to globalize in the 1960s, when retail, apparel, and electronics firms contracted suppliers in low-wage countries to meet a growing demand.[46] These industries remain significant as the first links of industrial supply chains, where they are subject to fierce competition among suppliers.

Much of this work relocated to China beginning in the 1990s. However, just as Chinese wages have risen—making countries like Vietnam and Bangladesh more industrially competitive—advances in robotics may finally be overcoming long-standing resistance to further mechanization within these fields. Capital accumulation is still unfolding at a more rapid pace in East and Southeast Asia, where much of this production takes place, meaning new inventions are more likely to be implemented as innovations in business practice. Foxconn is deploying "foxbots" on their electronics assembly lines to stave off competition from assemblers in lower-wage countries. In China and Bangladesh, apparel companies are using "sewbots," as well as new knitting technologies that have already been extended to the manufacture of "flyknit" footwear. These innovations are unlikely to lead to full automation in these sectors, but they could eliminate lots of jobs quickly and block access to the global economy for further low-wage countries, for example, in Africa.[47] It is unclear whether these technological developments are ten or twenty years away, and they may not occur on any scale at all. Yet even without major advances in automation, "Industry 4.0" and "smart factory" technologies may increase the advantages of industrial clustering in the vicinity of related services, with the result that manufacturing jobs are more likely to be globally concentrated than dispersed.[48]

By overcoming impediments to mechanization in sectors that have hitherto acted as major labor absorbers, new technologies may serve as a secondary cause of the underdemand for labor. However, the key to explaining this phenomenon is not the rapid pace of job destruction in these branches of production, but rather the absence of a correspondingly rapid pace of job creation in the wider economy. As I have argued, the main explanation for the latter is not runaway technological change, as the automation theorists claim, since that would show up in economic statistics as a rapid rate of productivity growth. In reality, productivity growth rates are slowing down, not speeding up. The low demand for labor in the wider economy finds its true source in the slackening pace of overall economic growth, associated with the running down of the manufacturing growth engine and the failure to find an alternative to it. The tendency toward economic stagnation will only intensify in the COVID-19 pandemic era.

It is for this reason that predictions of a coming wave of pandemic-induced automation ring so hollow. They mistake the technical feasibility of automation (itself more of a shaky hypothesis than a proven result) for its economic viability. Undeniably, some firms are investing in robotics in response to COVID-19. For example, Walmart has purchased self-driving, inventory scanning, and aisle cleaning robots for its US stores. Expecting online ordering to continue to expand exponentially, some retail shops are testing out—but not yet widely implementing—robotics assisted micro-fulfillment centers, to help pickers assemble orders more quickly.[49] However, these are likely to be exceptions to the rule for the foreseeable future. With little reason to expect the demand for their products to increase following the onset of a deep recession, few firms will undertake major new investments. Instead, firms will make do with the productive capacities they already possess: achieving cost savings by shedding labor and speeding up the pace of work for the remaining workers. That is precisely what firms did after the last recession. Too often, commentators simply assume that automation accelerated in the last decade and base their predictions for the future on this false reckoning of the past. The demand could not be found to justify such investments. In the United States, the 2010s saw the lowest rates of capital accumulation and productivity growth in the postwar era. COVID-19 will only tend to make things worse.

CHAPTER 4

A Low Demand for Labor

AT THE CORE OF the automation discourse is the concept of what economist Wassily Leontief called "long-run technological unemployment." Extrapolating from particular instances of automation-induced job loss, theorists claim to have discovered a general phenomenon: in the coming decades, full automation will supposedly lead to "full unemployment." Like "whale oil" and "horse labor," Erik Brynjolfsson and Andrew McAfee suggest in *The Second Machine Age*, human exertion may soon find itself "no longer needed in today's economy even at zero price."[1] Were full automation upon us, the resulting jobs apocalypse would quickly demonstrate that social life had to be reorganized so that waged work was no longer at its center.[2] The past two chapters cast doubt on this prediction, yet like the automation theorists, I too have argued that the world economy is beset by labor underdemand. Has this low labor demand been accompanied by rising unemployment rates, as the automation discourse suggests it should have?

Across the advanced capitalist economies, unemployment rates rose rapidly after the 2008 crisis, yet over the 2010s, those rates fell, although at a much slower pace than in the wake of past recessions (Figure 4.1). In 2020, unemployment levels spiked again due to the COVID-19 recession—in the US, they rose at unprecedented speeds—but that had little to do with automation. If the past is any guide to the future, unemployment levels will likely fall again, albeit at a slow pace, over the coming decade. Such data hardly fits with an account of rising long-run technological employment, but this should not be taken as evidence that the demand for labor has not declined. Under the pressure of decelerating economic growth, the mode in which labor underdemand expresses itself has shifted: from *un*employment to a variety of forms of chronic *under*employment, which are more difficult to measure.[3]

As many commentators have already recognized, we are heading toward a "good job–less future" rather than a "jobless" one. Workers typically lack the reserves that would allow them to live for long without earning a labor-based income. As automation theorist and former presidential contender Andrew Yang argues, "workers have to keep working in order to feed themselves, so they take any jobs in sight"— including jobs offering poor pay, limited hours, or terrible working conditions.[4] Automation theorists like Yang interpret this trend as a consequence of growing technological unemployment, occurring somewhere offstage. In reality, rapid automation has hardly taken place at all—offstage or anywhere else. Still, rates of job creation have fallen over the past half century, primarily due to ongoing slowdowns in average rates of economic growth. That has made it more difficult for workers who lose their jobs in the midst of downturns to find equivalent forms of work during the weak recoveries that follow. Many are discouraged from looking for work at all. Governments have generally responded to this persistently low demand for labor not by promoting work sharing among the employed, but rather by reducing workers' access to unemployment benefits—pushing job losers to take whatever work was available, even at the cost of lost wages and degraded skills.

Working at Any Cost

Starting in the 1970s, unemployment rates in wealthy countries began to rise from historically low levels. Outside of the United

Figure 4.1. Unemployment Rates in the US, Germany and Japan, 1960–2017

Source: OECD Main Economic Indicators, Unemployment Rate, Ages 15 and over.

States, they remained stubbornly high for decades.[5] In that context, unemployment insurance programs went into crisis: they had been designed for short bouts of cyclical unemployment in fast-growing economies, not long-term unemployment in stagnating economies. To coax the unemployed back to work, governments began to reduce labor market protections and scale back unemployment benefits. Active labor market policies replaced passive income-support systems as the main response to job loss.[6] In Denmark and Sweden, governments tried to balance inducements to work by spending almost 1 percent of GDP in 2016 on placement services, training programs, and employer incentives, but they achieved mediocre results in slow-growing economies. In most wealthy countries, such programs were even less in evidence: spending on active labor market policies (not including direct job creation) averaged just 0.3 percent of GDP in OECD countries in that same year.[7]

Under these conditions, few workers remain unemployed for long. No matter how bad labor market conditions become, they still have to try to find work, since they need to earn an income in order to live. As growing numbers of workers find themselves without reserves, the present-day world economy comes to look more like the one Marx analyzed in the mid nineteenth century, in *Capital*. In a stagnant economy, Marx explained, the stagnant portion of capitalism's "industrial reserve army" or "relative surplus population" will tend to grow. "Recruited from workers in large-scale industry and agriculture who have become redundant," this stagnant surplus population comes to form a "self-reproducing and self-perpetuating element of the working class," which takes "a proportionally greater part in the general increase of that class than the other elements." Since their work is "characterized by a maximum of working time and a minimum of wages," their "conditions of life" tend to "sink below the average normal level." The expansion of this population was, for Marx, an "absolute general law of capitalist accumulation."[8] Written over 150 years ago, Marx's analysis has become contemporary once again. In the slow-growing economies of the past few decades, job losers have been obliged to join new labor market entrants in low-quality jobs—earning less-than-normal wages in worse-than-average working conditions. Unlike in Marx's time, this phenomenon is mediated, today, by postwar welfare-state institutions, which have continued to shape labor-market outcomes even as those institutions have deteriorated over time. Cross-country institutional differences determine the degree to which experiences of precariousness diffuse through the workforce or remain concentrated within specific sections of the population.[9]

Such shifts are easiest to document in the United States, where only unionized workers are afforded basic employment protections. Almost all other employees are hired at will and, barring outright discrimination, can be fired at any time. Between 1974 and 2019, unemployment rates were on average 30 percent higher than they were between 1948 and 1973, primarily due to lower rates of job creation following recessions. Over the same period, private sector unionization rates declined significantly: from nearly 30 percent in the early 1970s to 6 percent in 2019. Firms were therefore able to take advantage of higher average unemployment rates, which left many workers fearing for their jobs, to put the squeeze on employees. Given the difficulty many workers would face finding new work were they fired from their jobs, they have been compelled to accept relatively stagnant real wages as the condition of working at all.[10]

Some economists have argued, on the contrary, that over the past few decades it is only US workers without college degrees who have truly faced deteriorating labor market conditions. In a less extreme version of the automation thesis, these economists claim that technological change has hollowed out the American job market, destroyed middle-wage jobs, and polarized employment opportunities between high- and low-wage work. The automation of routine tasks is said to have generated a rising college wage premium, setting off a race between education and the machines. It is certainly true that, in the United States, experiences of precariousness are strongly modulated for individual workers by education levels, as well as race. Unemployment levels in the United States are significantly higher for workers with low educational attainments and for people of color. It is also true that, in the 1980s and early '90s, some Americans were able to insulate themselves from downward pressure on wages by getting a college degree. However, by the early 2000s—when the automation of economic activity was supposed to be accelerating—the college wage premium had stabilized, since the wages of most college educated workers had begun to stagnate. The median American college-educated worker earned a lower real wage in 2018 than in 2000, even though the total value of outstanding student loans rose dramatically over those years. The reason is that from 2000 on, economic growth rates slowed significantly—and so too rates of job creation—while college degrees became more common: 40 percent of prime-age workers had at least a college degree in 2019. Those degrees offered less protection from deteriorating labor market conditions. Workers with college degrees crowded out workers with lower levels of educational attainment in jobs that did not previously require such degrees. Meanwhile, the share of young college-educated workers with employer-sponsored healthcare halved, from 61 percent in 1989 to 31 percent in 2012. Despite earning higher wages than their less educated counterparts, many of these workers were precariously employed.[11]

What makes the United States unusual, from an international comparative perspective, is precisely that experiences of economic precariousness diffuse throughout the workforce. Even regularly employed US workers find that they are highly exposed to potential job loss in a persistently low-labor-demand economy, since they can be fired at any time. The consequence is that, unlike firms in other countries, US firms face no particular need to construct alternative working arrangements to take advantage of vulnerable sections of the labor force. Some firms do utilize alternative working arrangements to get around US labor law—witness the small but significant boom in gig-economy jobs, like Uber and Lyft, which offer work through online platforms as a way of disguising their employees as independent contractors.[12] But when all is said and done, just 10 percent of US workers were employed in such arrangements in 2017, including as independent contractors, on-call workers, temp agency workers, and fixed-contract workers.[13]

Set against this American case, the employment landscape in European and wealthy East Asian countries is more complicated. In these regions, postwar labor market institutions were mostly designed not by left-wing governments but by right-wing politicians who emphasized the importance of national-imperial identities, the formation of male-breadwinner households, and the maintenance of relatively fixed workplace hierarchies.[14] In return for accepting corporatist arrangements, male heads of households received substantial job protections: unlike in the United States, regularly employed workers were not hired and fired at will. For a crude measure of the difference that has made, we can look to the OECD index of employment-protection levels, which measures, on a scale of 0 to 6, the degree to which employees are protected from individual firings. Permanent workers in the US barely register at all on this index (at 0.5), while workers in the UK (at 1.2), Japan (1.6), Germany (2.5), Italy (2.5), and France (2.6) have been much more protected (Figure 4.2).[15] In the latter countries, heads of households who obtained permanent jobs were largely insulated from market pressures associated with a declining demand for labor. They remained free to fight for collective wage increases, even as economy-wide unemployment rates rose to 10 percent or more. Meanwhile, as compared to the US, unemployed workers in these countries received more generous out-of-work benefits.

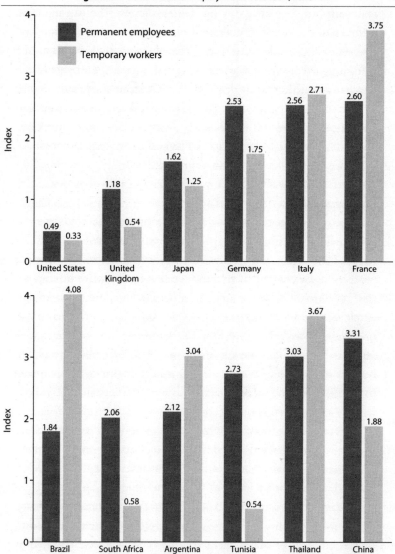

Figure 4.2. OECD Index of Employment Protection, 2013–14

Source: The OECD indicators of employment protection are synthetic indicators of the strictness of regulation on dismissals and the use of temporary contracts. They are compiled from 21 items covering three different aspects of employment protection regulations as they were in force on January 1.

In most high-income countries, rising rates of unemployment from the mid 1970s onward therefore did not initially cause workers' real wages to stagnate as in the United States. The workers who suffered most were the unemployed, as well as the children and spouses of still-employed workers. The jobs crisis took the form of a worsening exclusion; it was concentrated on specific sectors of the population rather than widely diffused. Older unemployed workers were pushed into early retirement. Married women were discouraged from looking for work, which is why women's labor force participation rates remained low in many European countries and Japan— with Sweden as a key exception—into the 2000s.[16]

Given employees' stronger holds over the jobs they possessed, European and East Asian firms needed to secure institutional changes in employment relations in order to take advantage of low levels of labor demand. Responding to pressure from employers, governments stripped job losers and new labor market entrants of employment protections by coaxing them into so-called nonstandard job categories: as part-time, temporary, or otherwise contractually limited employees. Some of these categories, like *Minijobs* in Germany, had previously been de facto reserved for housewives and were meant to serve as a secondary source of income, but have since grown to become primary sources of income for many households.[17] Compared to workers on standard employment contracts, nonstandard workers have fewer employment protections.[18]

The term "precarity" entered a wider lexicon precisely amid protests against laws that reduced job security for many workers, particularly for women and youth.[19] For instance, the 2003 Biagi law allowed Italian firms greater "flexibility" in firing part-time and temporary workers; the 2004 Hartz IV reforms substantially reduced out-of-work benefits in Germany. Similar efforts to strip young labor market entrants of employment security in France were rebuffed by workers in 2006 and again in 2016. Yet despite bouts of resistance, labor markets in western Europe and wealthy East Asia have become steadily more bifurcated between workers in standard employment with relative job security, and a growing mass of (mostly younger) workers in nonstandard jobs who lack it.[20] Between 1985 and 2013, the share of nonstandard employment in total employment rose: from 21 percent to 34 percent in France; from 25 to 39 percent in Germany; from 29 to 40 percent in Italy; and from 30 to 34 percent in the UK. In Japan, the "non-regular employment" share (a category similar to the nonstandard employment share) rose from 17 percent in 1986 to 34 percent in 2008, with similar trends unfolding in South Korea. Changes in the composition of employment were much more dramatic for new job offerings: 60 percent of jobs created in OECD countries in the 1990s and 2000s were nonstandard.[21]

More and more workers were exposed to employment insecurity at a time when, due to slowing rates of job creation in anemic economies, they would have trouble finding new employment were they to lose their jobs. These workers were forced to moderate their demands for wage increases. Across the OECD, real median wages rose by 0.8 percent per year between 1995 and 2013, even though labor productivity rose by 1.5 percent per year, leading to a significant upward redistribution of income (although one that was less intense than in the United States alone, where those rates were 0.5 and 1.8 percent respectively).[22]

Surplus Labor on the World Scale

The global South presents a mixture of European- and American-style cases, but taken to greater extremes than on either side of the Atlantic. On the one hand, postwar and postcolonial developmental states generally adopted labor laws that were similar to, or even stronger than, those operating domestically in former European metropoles. Turning to the OECD employment protection index, once again, shows that in Argentina (at 2.1), Brazil (1.8), and South Africa (2.1), permanent workers on standard employment contracts have had stronger employment protections than equivalent workers in the UK (1.2); while in China (at 3.3), India (3.5), Thailand (3.0), and Tunisia (2.7), such workers have been more protected than even equivalent workers in France (2.6). On the other hand, few workers have access to protected jobs—which are generally found only in government offices and large-scale industrial plants—so the vast majority of workers across the global South have been forced to find employment instead in a variety of nonstandard jobs, where they have fewer protections than the least protected US workers.

In Africa, Asia, and Latin America, the expansion of nonstandard employment became a major problem well before the onset of labor's global deindustrialization. In the 1950s and '60s, the demand for work had already far outstripped its supply, as rapidly expanding nonagricultural workforces searched for jobs in slow-growing import-substitution industries. To describe the burgeoning populations of urban street-sellers, micro-manufacturers, and bicycle-based transport services they encountered, labor force statisticians developed the new category of "informal sector employment."[23] In the 1980s and '90s, informal sectors expanded considerably, as country after country adopted disastrous market-opening structural adjustment policies at a time of heightened international competition.[24] Workers who lost their formally contracted jobs at large-scale enterprises and government offices—or saw their salaries slashed—were forced to join new labor market entrants in working informally, during what was in many countries a time of nearly unending economic crisis. Meanwhile, to take advantage of growing labor surpluses, firms schemed to replace protected, formal employees with informal workers, while at the same time lobbying governments to reduce formal job protections as a stimulus to economic recovery.[25]

Unlike most other global South countries, China saw rapid economic growth in the 1980s and '90s, yet China's economy relied more heavily on the creation of legally disadvantaged categories of workers than any other country. The *nonming gong*, working in urban centers but registered in rural areas, were categorically denied employment protections offered to other urban workers. Sewing shirts and assembling electronics in export-oriented manufacturing establishments, these workers were forced to relinquish any thought of demanding higher real wages, since their job security was so low and competition for their jobs was so high.[26]

The expansion of nonstandard employment has exposed gigantic numbers of people to intense job insecurity worldwide. Workers are especially insecure in global South regions, insofar as they mostly lack access to even rudimentary legal protections and unemployment benefits. Worldwide, barely one-fifth of unemployed workers received unemployment benefits in 2012.[27] Therefore, workers had to find new sources of income as quickly as possible when they lost their jobs, with the result that the global unemployment rate was just 4.9 percent in 2019, despite a widely recognized dearth of job opportunities. Most workers who've lost their jobs have had to work informally.[28] In fact, according to the International Labour Organization, only 26 percent of the global workforce had permanent employment of any kind in 2015, whether full or part time, leaving 74 percent to work either for employers on temporary contracts or else informally, without a contract but for an employer, or on their own account.[29]

In this regard, the term "nonstandard employment" is clearly a misnomer: the residue of a mid-twentieth-century dream of full employment that never became a global reality, least of all in the parts of the world where most people live.[30] What that means in practice is that—with the exception of a tiny minority of protected employees—workers around the world find themselves highly exposed to the ebbs and flows of the demand for labor. In an era of generally low labor demand, many workers fear that were they to lose their current jobs, they would have trouble finding new ones, since there are already so many other workers just like them—with their same skills and aptitudes—who are unemployed or underemployed and looking for work. Facing job insecurity, these workers are forced to accept relatively stagnant wages and poor working conditions. This condition is not primarily the result of recent developments in computer technologies. Instead, it follows from decades of overcapacity and underinvestment, which ran down the economic growth engine of the world economy (and did so at a time when global labor forces were still expanding). Unless there is a drastic shift in state policy, the COVID-19 recession will only intensify these trends in the years to come.

Postindustrial Doldrums

Unemployment levels have risen substantially due to the COVID-19 recession; however, given the shifts in labor-market regimes documented above, this unemployment will likely resolve itself, over time, into a variety of forms of underemployment.[31] Unable to remain out of work for long, people will find that they have no choice but to take jobs offering lower-than-normal wages or worse-than-normal working conditions. Those who cannot find any work at all will set up shop in the informal sector or else will drop out of the labor force entirely. Life in stagnant economies has come to be defined by intense employment insecurity—all the worse in recession years, like 2020—which has been artfully represented in recent science fiction dystopias, populated by a redundant humanity. Most people are scraping by, earning additional minutes of life one at a time, while the richest asset-owners have amassed such large quantities of capital that they are endowed with the monetary equivalent of immortality.[32] Since they cannot remain unemployed, what kinds of work do these surplus workers do?

From the mid '60s onward, as labor surpluses expanded globally, multinational firms began to engage in labor market arbitrage, playing suppliers off each other to obtain productive labor at low prices, which they then used to compete in oversupplied global markets. Industrial firms have taken advantage of employment insecurity not only in thousands of export-processing zones in low-income countries around the world, but also in the high-income countries, where they have moderated workers' wage demands by creating multitiered contracts or hiring workers outside the bounds of standard labor law. Yet only about 17 percent of the global labor force works in manufacturing, with an additional 5 percent in mining, transportation, and utilities.[33] The vast majority of the world's underemployed workers therefore end up employed in the heterogeneous service sector, which accounts for between 70 and 80 percent of total employment in high-income countries, and the majority of workers in Iran, Nigeria, Turkey, the Philippines, Mexico, Brazil, and South Africa.[34] The postindustrial economy we have inherited, finally on a world scale, is, however, rather unlike the one whose emergence the American sociologist Daniel Bell first predicted in 1973: instead of an economy of researchers, tennis instructors, and Michelin-rated chefs, ours is predominantly one of side-street barbers, domestic servants, fruit-cart vendors, and Walmart shelf stackers.[35]

The basic pattern of employment growth in services was best described by Princeton economist William Baumol in the 1960s. His theory helps explain why underemployment in the sector has been such a major feature of the twenty-first-century economy—and why the automation theorists' account falls askew.[36] Baumol explained rising service sector employment by pointing out that service occupations typically see much lower rates of productivity growth than the industrial sector. Services generally do not exhibit dynamic patterns of expansion, with output growing faster than productivity, which in turns grows faster than employment (as was the case in manufacturing before 1973). Instead, most output growth in services is generated by expanding employment (Figures 4.3 and 4.4). Echoing at a distance Marx's concept of the "stagnant" relative surplus population, Baumol argues that services come to form a relatively "stagnant" economic sector.[37] There is a clear link between the global expansion of this stagnant economic sector and the ever-worsening stagnation of the world economy.[38] In fact, to say so is merely to reiterate that, following the onset of labor's global deindustrialization, nothing—including in the expansion of service sector employment—has proven capable of serving as an adequate replacement for the economy's formerly robust industrial economic-growth engine.

That services are not amenable to the incremental process innovations that generate rapid rates of productivity growth is hardly an inherent feature of services as such: in many service activities, impediments to raising productivity levels have been overcome, but precisely by industrializing them. As sociologist Jonathan Gershuny has argued, these services were transformed into goods for self-service in households, "the washing machine substituting for laundry services, the safety-razor for barbershop shaving, the motorcar for public

Figure 4.3. Service Sectors in the US, France and Italy, 1980–2010

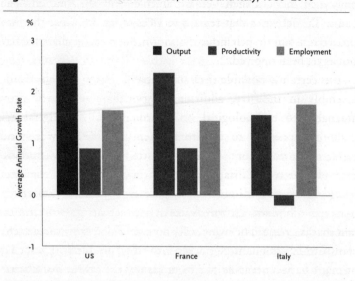

Figure 4.4. Service Sectors in Thailand, Mexico and South Africa, 1980–2010

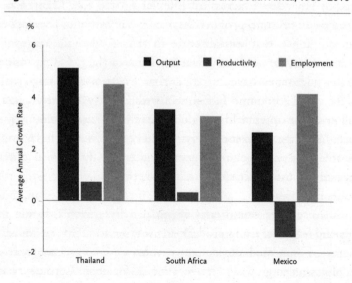

Source: Groningen Growth and Development Centre, 10-Sector Database, January 2015 edition.

transport."[39] Rendered via industrial processes, these goods-embodied services then became amenable to dynamic efficiency gains. The activities that remain services today are those that have proven resistant to such industrialization, due to resistances that have not as yet been resolved.[40]

It is certainly possible that, like apparel sewing and electronics assembly in industry, additional service activities will prove amenable to technological breakthroughs in the digital age, making it possible to transform them into self-service goods rendered via ever more efficient industrial processes. Witness, for example, the recent disappearance of travel agencies. However, it would be a grave mistake to imagine that the main barriers to dynamic economic growth in our times were merely technical, and that they could be overcome through technological leaps that transformed stagnant services into dynamic industries. The primary barrier remains the redundancy of technical capacities around the world, making for crowded global markets in which output rises slowly across all lines of production. Many mass-produced industrial products have come online since the start of labor's global deindustrialization in the 1970s (for instance, a large variety of consumer electronics), but if anything, these newer industries have suffered from worse overcapacity than older ones. The same fate would befall any self-service goods derived from present-day service activities. Then, as now, job losers and labor market entrants would be forced to look for work in whatever activities remain open, taking advantage of a key feature of those activities that makes them choice sites for underemployment.

Since services cannot rely on price effects for expansion of demand—that is, rising productivity leading to falling prices and hence to increased demand—we should expect service sector employment to grow slowly over time. As Baumol showed, service sector prices suffer from a "cost disease": sluggish rates of productivity growth mean that services become ever more expensive relative to goods.[41] Service sector demand must therefore rely on income effects for its expansion—the growth of demand for services depends on the growth of incomes across the wider economy. However, this means that as the rate of overall economic growth slows with the dilapidation of the industrial growth engine, the pace of service sector employment growth should slacken, too— and it generally has, across the advanced capitalist countries. But despite advanced economies' slower growth, service sector employment expanded steadily in certain occupations, in which legal-institutional frameworks had allowed for the hiring of precarious labor. It is precisely at this point that the logics of underemployment come into play.

It turns out to be possible to lower the prices of some services, and so to expand demand for them in spite of overall economic stagnation, without raising corresponding levels of productivity—that is, by paying workers less, or by suppressing the growth of their wages relative to whatever meager increases in their productivity are achieved over time.[42] Since difficulties in raising rates of productivity growth in these services are persistent, employers are incentivized to exert further downward pressure on wages, either to keep up with their competitors or to race ahead of them. The same principle applies to self-employed workers, who, by offering to work for less, are able to create demand for their labor at the expense of their incomes. The service sector is the choice site for job creation through such super-exploitation because the wages of service workers make up a relatively large share of the final price that consumers pay. Since labor productivity levels tend to be lower in services, it is often possible for small-scale family operations to compete with highly capitalized firms, as long as the former are successful in pushing their incomes down to a minimum. Particularly in low- and medium-income countries, productivity growth in many services has been negative, as people contrive work for themselves via involutionary job-creation strategies.

The extent to which firms are allowed to take advantage of income-insecure workers to generate immiserating forms of work, then, depends on the strength of each country's labor-protection laws. As we have seen, countries have generally intervened in low-labor-demand economies to reduce those protections. In fact, that was the explicit goal of the Organisation for Economic Co-operation and Development (OECD) itself, which has been a consistent advocate of labor flexibility as the way to bring down unemployment rates. By the late 1980s, OECD economists had come to recognize that, given slower economic growth rates, firms were unlikely to invest sufficiently to increase the capital stock in line with what was required to generate new high-productivity, high-wage jobs. It therefore seemed "inescapable" that "a reasonably rapid growth of employment would require the creation of many jobs which use a below-average amount of capital to support them, and for which—in consequence—the supportable real wage would be correspondingly modest." Looking to the United States, where unemployment rates fell because "the average real wage of the new jobs" was held "below the average real wage of existing jobs," the OECD began to advocate this perverse job-creation strategy everywhere.[43] OECD economists could never have foreseen that the period of economic stagnation would last this long. However, they should have predicted the socially dislocating effects that would follow from this policy.

As underemployment rises, inequality must intensify. Masses of people can only work as long as the growth of their incomes is suppressed relative to the average rate of income growth. As economists David Autor and Anna Salomons note, "Labour displacement need not imply a decline in employment, hours or wages," but can hide itself in the relative immiseration of the working class, as "the wage bill—that is, the product of hours of work and wages per hour—rises less rapidly than does value added."[44] The consequence is to further expand the gap between the average growth rate of real wages and of productivity levels—contributing to the 9-percentage-point shift from labor to capital incomes in the G20 countries over the past fifty years. Worldwide, the labor share of income fell by 5 percentage points between 1980 and the mid 2000s, as a growing portion of income growth was captured by a tiny class of wealth holders.[45]

As I discussed earlier, increases in inequality have been worse than even these statistics suggest, since the distribution of labor income has itself become more unequal, with the largest pay raises going to managers. Between the late 1980s and the early 2010s, labor productivity grew faster than average wages, which in turn grew faster than median wages across the OECD.[46] Over time, immiserating employment growth becomes self-reinforcing. Sectors of the economy expand by taking advantage of pools of underemployed labor and then come to depend on their continued availability. As thoughtfully depicted in Bong Joon-ho's award-winning 2019 film *Parasite*, it begins to make sense for high-net-worth and managerial households to hire working-class households to perform more of the tasks they would otherwise do for themselves—as tutors, domestic servants, drivers, childminders, and personal assistants—simply due to large differences in the prices of their respective labors.[47]

These trends suggest that the apocalyptic crisis of labor market dysfunction anticipated by automation theorists will not take place. Instead, unemployment will continue to spike during downturns—as we are seeing happen once again, and on a truly massive scale, in the present COVID-19 recession. Then, in the course of the tepid boom periods that follow, this unemployment will slowly but surely resolve itself into higher levels of underemployment and rising inequality. In *Rise of the Robots*, futurist Martin Ford says that his worst nightmare would be if the "economic system eventually manages to adapt to the new reality" of labor displacement. But in truth, it has. As Mike Davis put it, the "late-capitalist triage of humanity" has "already taken place."[48] Unless halted by concerted political action, the coming decades are likely to see more of the same: overcapacity in international markets for agricultural and industrial products will continue to push workers out of those sectors and into services, which will see their share of global employment climb from 50 percent today to 70 or 80 percent by mid century. Since overall rates of economic growth are set to remain low, the service sector will absorb job losers and new labor market entrants only by increasing income inequality, leading us further and further into the postindustrial doldrums.

This is not to say that the poor will get poorer. In fact, the share of the world's population suffering from the most extreme forms of poverty has declined over time, alongside the urbanization of the world's population.[49] However, poorer workers' share of overall income growth remains much smaller than their share of the population. As economist Thomas Piketty and his colleagues have shown, incomes for the poorest half of the global population doubled between 1980 and 2016 (though rising by only a tiny amount in absolute terms), but that accounted for only 12 percent of overall income growth; the richest 1 percent captured more than twice that share—27 percent—over the same period.[50] As inequality has risen, social mobility has fallen.[51] Whether working as home health aides in Minnesota, adjunct university lecturers in Italy, fruit vendors in Tunisia, or construction workers in India, more and more people feel that they are stuck in place. Young labor-market entrants earn incomes that could never support independent households, especially where rents are rising quickly. They are often unable to move out of their parents' homes and start families. Taking on debt in an effort to get ahead, they find that repaying their loans absorbs a large portion of their wages, since their incomes remain relatively stagnant over time.[52]

To struggle against the labor market forces that are making people so miserable would require a substantial shift in labor's capacity to press its interests. Yet over time, the organized sector of the labor force has receded. Union density across the OECD declined from 30 percent of the workforce in 1985 to 16 percent in 2016; the share of workers covered by collective bargaining fell from 45 percent to 32 percent over the same period.[53] Global union density fell even lower, weighing in at approximately 7 percent in 2014.[54] Under these conditions, the containment of economic inequality has come to depend more and more on the strength and generosity of welfare-state institutions. However, these too have tended to give way in the face of economic stagnation. In sluggish economies periodically wracked by austerity, it is easier to blame the resulting social deterioration on vulnerable sections of the workforce—immigrants, women, racial and religious minorities—than to unite around a new, emancipatory social project.

CHAPTER 5

Silver Bullets?

T HE AUTOMATION DISCOURSE HAS identified a set of troubling tendencies in the world economy associated with a persistently low demand for labor. The social crisis entailed by this long-unfolding trend has been worse than the statistics indicate. Growing numbers have found themselves excluded from meaningful participation in the economy and from the sense of agency and purpose that it affords, as limited as that may be under the adverse conditions of capitalist societies. Atomization, amplified by job insecurity and inequality, renders people susceptible to the appeal of economic nationalism, which claims to solve globalization's problems by putting "our country first."[1] Automation theorists are attentive to the dangers of nationalist solutions; a chronically low demand for labor will not be alleviated by tariff barriers or walled borders.[2] Measured against the catastrophes of the present era, such bromides offer little hope.

What other solutions are available? The automation theorists step into this breach like travelers from another time, or planet, offering a radical rethink. In this respect, automation is a lot like global warming: when people take it seriously, they find themselves willing to consider revisions to the basic structure of social life that they otherwise would have thought impossible. Naming the present world as obsolete allows automation theorists to boldly explore new, thought-provoking proposals for resolving the crisis of the world of work. These proposals are worth considering, even if, as I have been arguing, they are wrong about the causes of the crisis. In evaluating the automation theorists' recommendations, it is crucial to recall that today's persistently low demand for labor finds its true cause in decades of industrial overcapacity and the underinvestment to which it gives rise. A real solution must resolve this key issue.

Keynesianism Reloaded

To put the automation theorists' proposals into context, it is worthwhile to begin by considering one option they all dismiss, namely Keynesian interventions to induce higher levels of fixed capital investment, with the goal of soaking up the global labor surplus. As the automation theorists have described it, the world's labor crisis cannot be resolved by Keynesian means; job-destroying technical change, if it took the form of full automation, would be a problem no matter how fast the economy were growing. Since the low demand for labor is actually due to ongoing technological change in the midst of a persistent economic slowdown, Keynesian economic stimulus should be effective, were it possible to significantly raise economic growth rates on that basis. Why not take the Keynesian plunge? The truth is that governments in most high-income countries never stopped diving down that chasm.

Scholars tend to think of the 1970s as the end of the Keynesian era, but in many ways, it was just beginning. During the quarter century following the end of World War II, Keynesian counter-cyclical spending was actually little in evidence: instead of spending beyond their means, governments used the opportunity of galloping economic growth rates to reduce debt burdens they had incurred during the war (Figure 5.1). Between 1946 and 1974, the UK reduced its public debt-to-GDP ratio from 270 percent to just 52 percent, all while investing in education, healthcare, housing, transportation, and communication infrastructures.[3] Across the G20 countries, government debt-to-GDP ratios fell from 107 percent to 23 percent over the same period. This evidence hardly supports the view that full employment, when and where it was achieved in the postwar era, was the result of Keynesian demand stimulus.[4]

Instead, as I have argued in previous chapters, rapid postwar industrial expansion generated a consistently high and stable demand for labor largely on its own. Public spending on education, healthcare and infrastructural development did not stimulate private investment; the former could barely keep up with the latter's needs. More productive capacity came online after the end of World War II than ever before in world history. But precisely for that reason, international markets for manufactures quickly began to suffer from overcapacity, issuing in a reduced pace of capital accumulation and falling rates of output growth. The replication of technical capacities across the world undermined the conditions for further rapid expansion. The result was wave after wave of deindustrialization and a persistently low labor demand.

The era of counter-cyclical spending began in earnest in the 1970s, precisely in response to capital's disinvestment from the economy. Governments spent gigantic sums of money in an effort to induce additional investment. Between 1974 and 2019, public debt-to-GDP ratios correspondingly rose across the G20 countries: from 23 percent to 103 percent. In some countries, such as the United States (107 percent), Italy (135), and Japan (237), debt-to-GDP ratios in 2019 were even higher. With the exception of the UK, where debt levels stabilized from 1980 to 2007, states exhibited no tendency to wean themselves off deficit spending during the neoliberal era. Policymakers abandoned full employment as their goal, but facing ever more anemic economies, governments continued to take on large quantities of debt during downturns, only to find it difficult to raise additional tax revenue during the weak upturns that followed.[5]

The failure of debt-driven spending to stimulate high rates of economic growth should be all the more surprising, from a Keynesian perspective, given that long-term interest rates simultaneously fell to near zero. Falling interest rates should have encouraged investment in

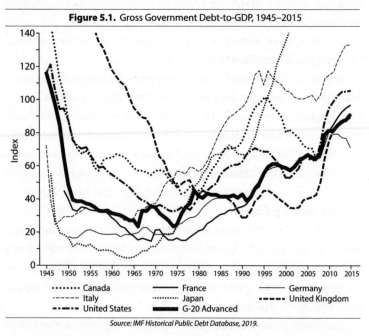

Figure 5.1. Gross Government Debt-to-GDP, 1945–2015

Canada ········ France —— Germany ——
Italy – – – Japan ········· United Kingdom ▬ ▬ ▬
United States ▬·▬·▬ G-20 Advanced ▬▬▬

Source: IMF Historical Public Debt Database, 2019.

fixed capital. Buoyed by ultralow interest rates, debt levels did rise dramatically among financial and nonfinancial corporations as well as private households. Total debt, both public and private, rose to record levels of 383 percent of GDP in the mature economies in 2019 (and 322 percent of GDP worldwide) before the COVID-19 recession hit.[6] Yet in spite of enormous debt accumulations, average annual economic growth rates continued to decelerate across the OECD: from 5.7 percent in the 1960s, to 3.6 percent in the 1970s, 3.0 percent in the 1980s, 2.6 percent in the 1990s, and 1.9 percent from 2000 to 2019.[7] Companies turned to debt financing not to invest in new fixed capital, but rather to engage in mergers and acquisitions, or to buy back their own stocks.[8] In the absence of any viable alternative to the industrial growth engine, the stimulation of demand has induced less and less new private investment. That bodes poorly for COVID-19 stimulus packages: like their predecessors, they too will fail to encourage a new wave of capital accumulation. In the absence of a revival of economic growth, states are likely to reimpose austerity once the pandemic ends.

Instead of trying to restart the growth engine via Keynesian stimulus, we need to rethink the framework we use to allocate people to production. Keynes himself would have agreed with that aim, although not with the means required to get there.[9] As capital accumulates "up to the point where it ceases to be scarce," Keynes argued, profit rates will fall to low levels, leading to the onset of a period of economic maturity, which Keynes's American counterpart Alvin Hansen called "secular stagnation."[10] Harvard economist Larry Summers has recently revived the secular stagnation thesis. He now claims that the austerity-induced "structural reform" he previously advocated is unlikely to lead the economy to health; instead, he argues, only massive "public investment" can restore full employment.[11] Keynes would have agreed with the need for greater public investment, but he would have argued, further, that the onset of economic maturity was an indication that the capitalist era was drawing to a close.

Under conditions of economic maturity, Keynes said, it would make more sense to intervene to *shrink the labor supply* rather than to *stimulate labor demand*, increasing leisure rather than output.[12] Given a long-term decline in returns to private investment, Keynes suggested, the work-week might have to be reduced to fifteen hours—and even that was only to satisfy the "old Adam" in us— that is, the need to feel useful.[13] Many economists misinterpret Keynes's vision as a quixotic prediction about workers' preferences with regard to future productivity gains: as if Keynes were saying that in the future, workers' stated preferences for increased vacation time, rather than rising wages, would cause working hours to shrink over the course of three generations.[14] By contrast, radical Keynesians like British economists Joan Robinson and William Beveridge knew that to get to the post-scarcity world of Keynes's dreams, it would be necessary to socialize investment levels and legislate shorter working days.[15]

Beveridge's 1944 plan for "full employment in a free society" (which he released shortly after his design for the British National

Health Service met with public acclaim) proposed to do just that. Beveridge budgeted for twenty-two more years of capitalist development after the end of World War II: two years for a transition from war to peace and twenty years of "reconstruction," during which public investment would be mobilized to defeat the four "social evils of Want, Disease, Ignorance and Squalor." On this advanced social foundation, he argued, the state could begin to wind down the economy sometime in the late 1960s, increasing "leisure" to reduce weekly hours of work and favoring an "equitable distribution" of income to reduce levels of economic inequality.[16] Add to this program a planned transition from fossil fuels to renewable sources of energy, and Beveridge's proposal would rival the most radical designs for a Green New Deal today.[17] Of course, governments never seriously considered implementing Beveridge's full employment proposal. Examining the reasons for the failure of the radical Keynesian projects of the past shows why similar plans will hardly fare better today.

In the aftermath of World War II, proposed public-investment-led full employment programs were forcefully combatted and soundly defeated, at a time when left-wing organizations were much stronger than they are today (of course, most of those left-wing organizations were fighting for more than public investment: many were calling for the socialization of production).[18] Large asset-owners understood, correctly, that public investment posed an existential threat to their prerogatives regarding where and how much of society's resources to invest in the expansion of production—and hence whether economies would expand or slide into recessions.[19] It was not so much full employment they feared, but rather full employment achieved via public investment, which would have neutralized the capacity of large asset owners to throw society into chaos through threats of disinvestment. Throughout the postwar period and into the present, capitalists have ensured that they retained a tight grip over this heavy artillery of the class conflict: the capital strike.[20] By threatening to disinvest, capitalists have ensured that the private investment decisions of large firms are respected, as the condition of maintaining or restoring high levels of employment. Today, firms' grip over the capital-strike weapon is stronger than it was before, since investment levels are depressed and underemployment is widespread. Moreover, in a world where private investment is weak, fear that public investment could displace its private equivalent as the main driver of economic activity becomes all the stronger, since so little investment is taking place overall. It is a mistake to imagine that capitalists would ever agree to their own planned obsolescence.

To challenge capitalists' control over investment decisions, even under the guise of a New Deal–style capital-labor accord, is not a compromise. As Oskar Lange pointed out in 1938, "To retain private property and private enterprise and to force them to do things different from those required by the pursuit of maximum profit would involve a terrific amount of regimentation of investment," upsetting "the financial structure of modern capitalist industry" and encouraging firms "to use their economic power to defy the government authorities (for instance, by closing their plants, withdrawing investment, or other kinds of sabotage)."[21] Facing potential insubordination from powerful actors, radical Keynesians would need to threaten firms with full socialization. In order to make good on those threats, they would need to have already developed and disseminated a clear plan for doing away with private enterprise. But then, to have any chance of securing their aims, radical Keynesians would also need to have won the backing of major social movements. Only movements that presented a truly existential threat to asset owners' wealth would be able to bring capital to heel. Yet if those social movements were powerful enough to force capital to submit to a public-investment-driven economy, why would they not demand more? Such movements would not willingly allow for power's further concentration in the hands of the state (instead, they would demand a devolution of power to democratic organs of the people themselves). As we will see, automation theorists' UBI proposals suffer from a similar failure to reckon with the weapons capital wields, above all in an era of economic slowdowns. Capital disinvestment neuters all worker-empowering policies as soon as they are born.[22]

Free Money

Like the radical Keynesians, the automation theorists want to wind down the economy. However, they propose a different way to get there: not by raising levels of public investment and legislating a progressive reduction in the work-week, but rather by distributing no-strings-attached incomes to every citizen, without exception.[23] Set at a high enough level, this universal basic income would end poverty outright. It would also provide workers in insecure employment with a measure of security—a crucial reform in an era of mass underemployment. Advocates argue that UBI would also do much more, renewing society at a deeply moral level: by showing that there is a shared investment in each individual's thriving, a UBI would restore our sense of social solidarity. Governments in Spain and Scotland, as well as Democrats in the United States, have been weighing the idea of implementing emergency, minimal UBI programs due to COVID-19, which could then be made permanent once the pandemic ends.[24]

In a country like the United States, where racism birthed welfare programs that treat the poor with suspicion, if not contempt, a transition from means-tested benefits to universal ones would be a welcome move toward justice in itself. Meanwhile, in lower-income regions such as sub-Saharan Africa, UBI could make possible new welfare programs to service the poor without requiring states to build complex means-testing infrastructures.[25] Debates within the UBI camp concern whether UBI payments should be higher or lower, whether they should be taxed back from high-income earners, whether they should supplement or replace other welfare-state programs, and whether they should be extended widely or restricted to citizens.[26]

For the automation theorists, UBI resolves the central conundrum of their vision—how to provide people with an income, to price their preferences, in a world where human labor has been rendered largely or even fully obsolete. UBI is the technical solution that transforms the nightmare scenario of automation into the dream of post-scarcity. On this basis, automation theorists often present UBI as a neutral policy instrument—appealing to left and right—that solves the problem of global un- and underemployment, just as the Green Revolution technologies were supposed to solve the problem of global hunger. There is an inner affinity between technological determinism, which is the core of the automation discourse, and its recourse to technocratic solutions. Both positions elide difficult social and political questions by transforming them into putatively objective facts.

Such technocratic neutrality is a fantasy: depending on the manner in which it is implemented, UBI will lead in radically different directions, most of which will not bring us closer to a world of human flourishing.[27] A critique of the automation discourse's market-based vision of post-scarcity will help reveal the contours of a nonmarket alternative.

UBI proposals long predate the advent of the automation discourse. Some trace their origin to Thomas Paine, who suggested as early as 1797 that a lump-sum payment should be distributed to all individuals on reaching the age of majority.[28] Paine justified this coming-of-age grant along classically Lockean lines, arguing that all land had originally been held in common but had since been divided up into parcels of private property. Rising generations were therefore unable to access their fair shares of humanity's inheritance. For Paine, coming-of-age grants could serve as the cash equivalent of each person's share in the common stock of the earth—and thus enable everyone to participate in the world of private property. In his proposal, which anticipates the concept of basic income, payments are not a way to create a post-scarcity world, but rather to secure the moral foundations of a private-ownership society.

Twentieth-century neoliberal economists supported a basic income for similar reasons. Both Friedrich Hayek and Milton Friedman advocated for UBI, in the form of a negative income tax, as a replacement for welfare programs: instead of funding public projects aimed at reducing poverty, people should be given enough money to raise them above the poverty line.[29] This proposal was of a piece with Friedman's larger neoliberal worldview.[30] Instead of trying to resolve market failures by supplementing private activity with public activity—public education, healthcare, housing, regulations on pollution, and so forth—Friedman argued that states should bring more aspects of life within the purview of the price mechanism. He saw the market as the very foundation of freedom, responsibility, and self-respect. On this view, the poor did not need public assistance; they needed money, so that they could reimmerse themselves in markets.

Today, the most fulsome right-wing arguments for UBI are to be found in the writings of the infamous racist social critic Charles Murray, who has taken up Friedman's baton. In Murray's view, UBI will not only end poverty; he believes it will also halt the decline of the West, restoring its tired souls to Christian faith and monogamous marriage. Murray is responsible for the idea that UBI should be set at $1,000 per month—a sum chosen not because it would allow individuals to meet their basic needs, but rather because it represents the current cost of welfare-state programs. Murray's proposal is simply to liquidate the present-day welfare state and distribute its funds directly to the population as handouts.[31]

As is typical of many recent books by advocates of UBI, the latest edition of Murray's *In Our Hands* does say that UBI is needed now more than ever as a response to automation. But in truth, Murray's advocacy of UBI is only loosely based on the automation discourse.[32] His advocacy of UBI stems from his belief that welfare-state institutions are not only economically inefficient but soul-destroying: they entail the alienation to the state of essential sources of individual meaning-making, with the result that people neither know nor care for one another, and that they cannot truly be happy. Murray argues instead that social problems like poverty and drug addiction need to be handled directly by the communities in which they arise, through "voluntary associations" ensconced in moral worlds of faith and community values. UBI would support the formation of such associations by dismantling the institutions that presently shoulder these burdens and by providing individuals with a social wage to free up their time.[33]

A key feature of this right-wing proposal is that it is in no way designed to combat economic inequality. Murray suggests that further income redistribution be blocked by constitutional amendment, so that inequality could continue to rise after a UBI program had been implemented. Murray's proposal for UBI is a disturbing vision of how an ever more unequal society, marked by a persistently low demand for labor, might render this situation palatable to the poorer among its members, while at the same time freeing well-heeled market participants to enrich themselves without limit.[34] A clear danger is that, in its implementation, UBI will come to look more like this right-wing version than it does left-wing alternatives. And indeed, Murray's version of UBI is the one most discussed in Silicon Valley; correspondingly, it is also the one that inspires most of the automation theorists discussed in this book.

What, then, about the left-wing alternatives? One key difference is that the latter would be much more expensive, because they would aim to provide people with enough money to support a modicum of a good life. From a center-left egalitarian position, Philippe van Parijs, perhaps UBI's most widely respected advocate, wants to provide people with enough money to meet their basic needs, without dismantling the welfare state. He and Yannick Vanderborght aim at 25 percent of GDP per capita—roughly $40,000 annually per household in the United States. To make this palatable, they recommend starting payments at a "modest level" and not on a universal basis. Instead of busting down the political front door, UBI will likely have to "enter through the back door," they say, with a "participation condition," such as a community-service requirement, and eligibility restrictions to prevent "selective immigration" to UBI countries.[35]

Left-wing proponents of UBI claim that small beginnings presage big future gains in freedom, since even a modest monthly payment will begin to revitalize communities.[36] Their argument therefore mirrors its right-wing counterpart: both suggest that with the extension of UBI, voluntary associations will flourish. The difference between the left and the right versions of this argument is that the right envisions proliferating churches and rotary clubs, whereas the left envisions a strengthening of worker or consumer cooperatives and trade unions, as well as of collective care organizations and community gardens. By organizing the unorganized, low levels of UBI provide the social basis for a powerful push for higher levels of UBI, or alternatively, for higher wages, and hence for greater levels of overall economic equality.[37]

Left-wing proponents of the automation discourse take this UBI proposal and push it to extremes. For anti-capitalist automation theorists like Nick Srnicek and Alex Williams, a high UBI is precisely what is needed to facilitate a shift toward full *un*employment.[38] Basing their argument on an article coauthored by a younger, more radical van Parijs—titled "A Capitalist Road to Communism"— Srnicek and Williams claim that as automation advances, the value of the UBI should grow, until the power to purchase all goods and services is provided by this alternative distribution mechanism. That would not only mark a radical advance in equality; at its limit, it would lead to life beyond wage labor. In their *Inventing the Future*, UBI accomplishes even more: acting as a red wedge, it becomes a way to accelerate the transition to a fully automated world. A high minimum-income floor empowers workers to refuse work, which in turn incentivizes employers to make jobs enjoyable, or to automate them out of existence.[39] UBI becomes a means not of stabilizing the late-capitalist economy, but of pushing toward a post-scarcity world, in which the "economic problem" has been solved and people are free to pursue their passions. Past that point, the major questions concern humanity's ultimate horizon. Does freedom from work mean indulging in hobbies, as Keynes imagined? Or does it mean building space-ships and exploring the stars, as depicted in the science-fiction novels of Iain M. Banks?[40]

Limitations

In its liberal egalitarian forms, UBI has many attractive aspects. Even a minimal net redistribution can be welcomed on its own terms, above all if it goes some way to alleviate the stress of poverty and its associated mental and physical ailments. Combined with a global carbon tax, UBI could play a role in mitigating climate change, freeing us to cleave toward a carbon-neutral economy without worrying about the balance of jobs gained and lost in the course of a harrowing energy transition.[41] To evolve from a technocratic fix to an emancipatory social project, however, UBI would have to empower individuals to fight for dramatic and lasting social change. There are reasons to doubt that UBI will have that effect.

Let's begin with the flourishing communities that UBI proponents invoke. On the grounds of analytic consistency alone, the right-wing version of this argument makes more sense than the left. According to the right-wing advocates of UBI, bonds of social solidarity have been broken because human powers were alienated to state institutions; dismantling the welfare state should encourage those bonds to re-form. By contrast, the left has always argued that the alienation of human powers to capital is at least as important as their alienation to the state. After all, most of our needs are served today not by public bureaucracies, but by private ones: gigantic firms produce a myriad of goods for consumption by discrete households units.[42] Modes of transportation, communication, nourishment, and entertainment have all been transformed in line with this inner logic of the market. People spend hours a day in traffic on their way to or from work—together but fundamentally alone—sitting in their cars, eating McDonald's, and scrolling through cat videos on their phones. Social media apps were supposed to solve the epidemic of loneliness and social isolation, but studies have shown that they only make that problem worse.[43] In densely populated urban areas, COVID-19 pushed this capitalist logic to the extreme. Individuals retreated into their homes, ordering whatever household items they needed online, while powerful companies set about reorganizing supply chains and mobilizing masses of workers—whose jobs suddenly involved substantial new and under-remunerated risks—for contactless delivery.[44] As these examples underscore, economies that are already designed to reduce everyone to an atomic existence could easily accommodate UBI.

What of the further claim that UBI would empower workers in confrontations with their bosses? In fact, this is putting the cart before the horse: to win a UBI large enough to alter social relations, workers would first need to be empowered. A deeper concern is that even if UBI did give people a greater capacity to stand and fight, it is not clear that it presents a viable pathway toward broader emancipatory goals. For UBI to serve as the basis of a left-wing vision of exit from capitalism, the automation theorists' analysis would need to be correct: today's low labor demand would have to originate in rapidly rising productivity levels, associated with a fast pace of economic change. Were that the case, the main issue society would confront would be one of reorganizing distribution, not production, with rising economic inequality rectified by distributing more and more income as UBI payments. But if, as I have argued, contemporary underdemand for labor is the result of global overcapacity and depressed investment— driving down rates of economic growth—then such a distributional struggle would quickly become a zero-sum conflict between labor and capital, blocking, or at least dramatically slowing, progress toward a freer future. As such, we would need a plan for wresting control of the economy away from asset owners. Yet UBI proposals say little about how to reduce capital's sway over production.[45]

While UBI has the laudable goal of separating the income people earn from the amount of work they do, it would do nothing to alter the relation between income and assets, keeping us tethered to a system in which a sizable fraction of total income derives from interest (from extending credit), rent (from leasing land or homes), and profit (from running businesses). In other words, UBI would empower workers without disempowering capital, providing people more autonomy in the fulfillment of their "animal functions" but no greater role in shaping the wider social conditions under which they do so.[46] The profit motive would therefore remain the driving force of the economy, since large asset-owners would retain their power over investment decisions, which would continue to determine whether the economy grows or shrinks. Here, radical advocates of UBI would confront the same impasse as the radical Keynesians. Capital would continue to wield the weapon of the *capital strike*—the prerogative of owners of capital to throw society into chaos via disinvestment and capital flight. For forty years, in an environment of worsening overcapacity and slowing economic growth, capitalists have threatened the use of this weapon to force political parties and trade unions alike to capitulate to their demands: for looser business regulations, laxer labor laws, slower-growing or stagnant wages, and, in the midst of economic crises, private bailouts and public austerity.

A left that wants to use UBI to usher in a different sort of world would therefore need to present us with its Meidner Plan, bringing about the progressive socialization of the means of production via a planned transfer of asset ownership to society at large.[47] The problem is that it was precisely the threat of capital disinvestment during the crisis of the 1970s that led to the abandonment of the original Meidner Plan in Sweden. Such a plan would be even harder to realize today, when mass working-class organizations are much weaker and economic growth slower. A capital strike against efforts to raise a modest UBI to a higher level would quickly push the economy into crisis, forcing UBI advocates to press forward toward the post-scarcity world long before they were ready to make the leap, or else to back down. Facing such a *salto mortale*, reform parties typically have blinked.[48] For this reason, it is much easier to imagine that a UBI would stabilize at a low level, as a support of an ever more stagnant and unequal society built around private property, than that it would serve as a planetary highway to a world of free giving.

The ubiquitous decline in aggregate labor demand around the world, especially when combined with imminent environmental threats, has made it impossible to outgrow, economically speaking, the world's surplus labor problem. At the same time, slowing rates of economic growth, which underpinned this problem in the first place, have resulted in a situation in which capitalists fight ferociously against any reforms that threaten their control over investment decisions. This is the world we have inherited, and it is where our political reflections must begin. Only a conquest of production, which finally succeeds in wresting the power to control investment decisions away from capitalists, hence rendering the capital strike inoperative, can clear the way for us to advance toward a post-scarcity future.

CHAPTER 6

Necessity and Freedom

EVEN IF ONE DOUBTS automation theorists' account of technological progress—as I certainly do—their attempt to imagine and chart a path toward a post-scarcity future remains their thought's most attractive aspect, because it allows us to pose the question of how the pieces of this defunct world can be reassembled into a new mode of social existence. Harboring such a vision is crucial if we are to revive an emancipatory project today, not least because its future realization seems so far away. Nineteenth-century socialists knew they were far from achieving their goals, but they were nevertheless possessed by an idea of a freer future, which animated their struggle and the risks they took in its name. As late as 1939, poet and playwright Bertolt Brecht could still write: "Our goal lay far in the distance / it was clearly visible."[1] Few would say that today.

Not only are we living in an era of stubbornly entrenched neoliberalism, provoking angry ethno-nationalisms and climate-induced catastrophes of growing frequency and scale. We also lack a concrete idea of a real alternative. Central planning turned out to be both economically irrational and ecologically destructive, filling warehouses with shoddy products and proving susceptible to autocratic bureaucratization. European welfare states and Keynesian full-employment policies proved unable to adapt to a context of slowing growth and ongoing deindustrialization.[2] Meanwhile, against the attacks of neoliberals, social movements have mostly mustered rearguard defenses, which will merely slow our slide into the abyss.

So, "demand the future," indeed.[3] But which one? It is striking that *Star Trek: The Next Generation* provides the go-to example of a freer future for so many automation theorists. In this series reboot, launched in the late 1980s, a technology called the "replicator"— essentially a highly advanced three-dimensional printer—brings about the end of economic scarcity, allowing people to live in a world without money or markets.[4] Citizen-scientists are then free to explore the galaxy, "boldly going where no one has gone before," without having to worry about how they are going to earn a living. The question is: Can we envisage a post-scarcity world without the replicators—that is, even if full automation turns out to be a dream?

By focusing on technological progress rather than the conquest of production, automation theorists end up largely abandoning what has been seen as the basic precondition for generating a post-scarcity world, from Thomas More's 1516 *Utopia* to present-day Trekonomics. This precondition is not the free distribution of money, as the most recent wave of automation theorists have it, but rather the abolition of private property and monetary exchange in favor of planned cooperation.[5] One of the reasons they relinquish this key objective is that they begin from the wrong transitional questions: they start from the assumption that full automation will be achieved, going on to ask how we would need to transform society in order to save humanity from mass joblessness and create a world of generalized human dignity. It is possible to reverse this thought experiment. Instead of presupposing a fully automated economy and imagining the possibilities for a better and freer world created out of it, we could *begin* from a world of generalized human dignity, and then consider the technical changes needed to realize that world.

The Post-scarcity Tradition

What if everyone suddenly had access to enough healthcare, education, and welfare to reach their full potential? A world of fully capacitated individuals would be one in which every single person could look forward to developing their interests and abilities with full social support. What would have to change in the present for this future scenario to materialize? In a fully capacitated world, everyone's passions would be equally worthy of pursuit. Particular individuals would not be assigned to collect garbage, wash dishes, mind children, till the soil, or assemble electronics for their entire lives, just so others could be free to do as they please. Instead of pushing some people down "under the mudsill" in order to raise up the rest, as the South Carolina slave owner James Henry Hammond once put it, we would need to find another way to allocate the necessary labors that serve as the foundation for all our other activities.[6]

Whereas automation theorists place their hopes in technology, many of the original theorists of post-scarcity—such as Karl Marx, Thomas More, Étienne Cabet, and Peter Kropotkin—did not need to call on a *deus ex machina* to solve this riddle. They claimed that post-scarcity was possible without the automation of production. Instead, they argued, we needed to reorganize social life into two separate but interrelated spheres: a realm of necessity and a realm of freedom.[7] The distinction between these two realms comes from ancient Greece, although for Aristotle, this distinction was one between persons. Slaves were condemned to the realm of necessity, while only citizens were allowed to enter the realm of freedom. Aristotle was himself a reverse automation theorist, justifying slavery by reference to the absence of self-moving machines: "If every tool, when summoned, or even of its own accord, could do the work that befits it," he said, "then there would be no need either of apprentices for the master workers, or of slaves for the lords."[8] For Aristotle, the absence of such machines made servitude unavoidable.

Although his vision was not devoid of slaves, who were adorned with "golden chains," More transformed this division between classes into a division internal to the life of each individual. Drawing inspiration from Plato's *Republic* and the early Christians—who lived according to the principle of *omnia sunt communia*, or everything held in common—More had the inhabitants of his imagined island, Utopia, abolish money and private property. "Wherever there is private property" and "everything is measured in terms of money," he explained, "it is hardly possible for the common good to be served with justice and prosperity, unless you think justice is served when all the best things go to the worst people or that happiness is possible when everything is shared among very few, who themselves are not entirely happy, while the rest are plunged in misery." Living in a time of early agrarian capitalism, More was disgusted by the enclosures, by which farmers were "stripped of their possessions, circumvented by fraud, or overcome by force" in order to make way for the pasturing of sheep. Left with no option but to steal their daily bread, poor people were imprisoned or summarily executed. Instead of this patently absurd and cruel system, in which some were condemned to poverty and death so that others might be wealthy, More advocated the pooling of necessary labors in common and the opening up of a realm of freedom for all to enjoy. Indeed, in *Utopia*, "the commonwealth is primarily designed to relieve all the citizens from as much bodily labor as possible, so that they can devote their time to the freedom and cultivation of the mind." The class of idlers—Aristotle's free men—would be disbanded, so that everyone could have a share of idle time for themselves.[9]

Almost three hundred years later, these ideas inspired the exiled Rousseauian republican Étienne Cabet, who read More's *Utopia* in the British Museum and was immediately converted to the social ideal of post-scarcity. He wrote his own treatise, titled *Travels in Icaria* (1840), advocating for what he called "the community of goods."[10] To More's call for the abolition of money and private property, Cabet added the application of advanced machinery to reduce the extent of the labors of necessity. These were the ideas that inspired the French communists of the early 1840s, to whom Marx turned when he outgrew the liberal republicanism of his youth.[11] Marx condemned the French egalitarian communists—the followers of François-Noël Babeuf—for their asceticism. He rarely referred directly to Cabet, who had become a Christian mystic by the time Marx and Engels penned the *Communist Manifesto*. Nevertheless, Marx saw it fit to lift the famous slogan that would grace the communist banner—"From each according to his abilities, to each according to his need"—almost directly from *Travels in Icaria*'s "To each according to his needs, from each according to his strength."[12] Many of Marx's post-scarcity ideas are derived from his Morist predecessors.[13]

Marx then went beyond More and Cabet in charging that the post-scarcity world at which these thinkers aimed could only be achieved through mass action: it would not be handed down from on high by a wise lawgiver (as was the case in the visions of Plato, More, Rousseau, and Cabet). That was why the Paris Commune was so inspiring to Marx.[14] In the brief life of the Commune, workers invented new modes of democratic self-government, replacing periodically elected officials with immediately recallable delegates. Exiles from the defeated Commune, including Élie Reclus, later roamed Europe, coming into contact with revolutionaries like Peter Kropotkin, who went on to write detailed accounts of how democratically organized post-scarcity societies could be constructed. Kropotkin emphasized the role of voluntary associations in post-scarcity life. He argued that voluntary associations would flourish in a world where money and private property had been abolished and necessary labors were pooled in common.[15]

These ideas were taken up in various guises by Otto Neurath—the original target of the socialist calculation debate—and by thinkers as diverse as W.E.B. Du Bois, John Dewey, and Karl Polanyi. All advocated for a world in which democratic associations of women and men replaced the rule of markets with cooperative production, and— taking advantage of capitalist technologies—reduced the common labors of necessity to expand a realm of individual freedoms. Du Bois estimated that, in the "future industrial democracy," just "three to six hours" of necessary labor per person "would suffice," leaving "abundant time for leisure, exercise, study, and avocations." Instead of making some engage in "menial service" so that others might make art, he said, we would "all be artists and all serve." To many people, this vision of post-scarcity was what "socialism" and "communism" had come to mean, before their later identification with Stalinist central planning and breakneck industrialization.[16] I will take each component of this vision in turn, in order to sketch an account of how, on the basis of a conquest of production, fully capacitated individuals might solve the contemporary problem of persistent underdemand in a socially emancipatory direction.

Cooperative Justice

In the realm of necessity, we would share out the labors necessary for our collective reproduction, which form the condition of possibility of everything else we want to do. The precise extent of these labors would not be determined a priori—and so would need to be decided democratically—but would include the provision of all the goods and services necessary to make a life (the provision of housing, food, clothing, common intermediate and final goods, sanitation, water, electricity, healthcare, education, child and elder care, means of both communication and transportation, and so on). Theorists of post-scarcity generally estimate that these common labors would take anywhere from three to five hours a day—about one-third to one-half of a standard workweek—although this work could be concentrated in certain portions of each week or in specific years of life. Besides labor hours, other measures could also be used for social accounting. We would divide up responsibilities while taking into account individual aptitudes and proclivities. Some tasks would need to be performed locally, but many could be planned on a regional or global scale, using advanced computer technologies.

Of course, much necessary work is difficult to share out widely because it requires specialized skills: we would still need farmers, construction workers, surgeons, electricians, and machinists—though in a fully capacitated world, these specialisms would themselves be more evenly distributed. Utopian writer Edward Bellamy proposed one way to organize the division of labor in a post-scarcity society in his novel *Looking Backward* (1888). There, the supply and demand for labor determine how many hours people work, rather than how high a salary they earn. Skilled work is rewarded with a lesser labor contribution rather than higher pay, while the performance of risky or especially difficult labors earn an honorific—a kind of celebrity. As across societies today, which differ in their institutional preferences for general education or vocational training, there need not be a single solution to this problem, as long as the division of labor neither leaves important tasks undone, nor reproduces an elite class of technicians.[17]

The result of such work sharing would be that more people, including those currently cast aside as redundant workers, would participate in necessary work, so that the amount any one person had to do would be correspondingly reduced. Allowances would obviously be made for the differently abled as well as to let everyone take long periods off of work entirely: for rest, for travel, for grief, or for cultural immersion. In order to share such necessary labors at all, their character would need to be dramatically transformed. Social distinctions between waged and unwaged work, which have historically consigned women to the "hidden abode" of household production, would have to be abandoned. Moreover, production and consumption would need to be conceived as a closed loop, rather than end points cut off from other social-ecological considerations.[18] Coordination among fabricators, farmers, cooks, cleaners, engineers, and artists could then become the basis of new forms of "communal luxury."[19]

Once this initial metamorphosis is complete, the question remains as to how a fully capacitated humanity might further transform their common labors. Here, it is important to recall that technologies developed in capitalist societies are not neutral: they are designed to embody capitalist control, not to free humanity from drudgery. Nevertheless, we already have the technical wherewithal to make many tasks more enjoyable than they currently are. Rather than serving the uses of an owner class, such know-how might instead be applied to break down distinctions between skilled and unskilled labor, or to eliminate some kinds of labor altogether. In any case, such questions would be settled by human beings' collective determination of what they want to do, rather than decided for us by supposedly unstoppable technological forces. Instead of seeking to end our obligations to one another, which for automation theorists serves as the foundation of a world of generalized human dignity, the point would be to recognize and transform those obligations. To say so is not to champion the work ethic; it is to recognize that a free existence can be achieved right now, even if drudgery has not and never will go away. Dis-alienating community life—by taking that life under democratic control and collective care—becomes the way to ensure that individual freedom is shared by all.[20]

Note that what I am here calling necessary or reproductive labor is not necessarily unsatisfying, especially if it is apportioned in such a way that no one's life is entirely dominated by it. Minding children, for example, is not only good for children, but for adults too, opening them to the wonders of a child's experience of the world. Likewise, making dinner or washing dishes, when done collectively, can facilitate the formation or deepening of relationships (and when done alone, may help get us out of our heads). Whether a fully capacitated humanity would prefer such activities to be performed by food replicators and cleaning drones, so that people can get on with their scientific research unimpeded, remains to be seen.

In the post-scarcity tradition, the reorganization of necessary labors makes possible a world of free giving. Everyone can go to the social storehouses and service centers to get what they need, while—as More put it—"giving absolutely nothing in exchange."[21] All are therefore entitled to food, drink, clothes, housing, healthcare, education, means of transportation and communication, and so on, irrespective of their contribution to the labor of necessity, "just as all men" are "entitled to warm themselves in the heat of the sun"—although ecological sustainability would set constraints on their provision.[22] People could hop on a train, stop in at the local canteen, get their teeth cleaned, drop off children at day care, enroll in vocational courses, or find a place to sleep for the night without having to prove that they qualify for access. There would be no possibility of excluding someone from these social goods.

For a post-scarcity society to come into being, a literal cornucopia is not required. It is only necessary that scarcity and its accompanying mentality be overcome, so people can live, as More said, "with a joyful and tranquil frame of mind, with no worries about making a living."[23] According to this perspective, abundance is not a technological threshold to be crossed. Instead, abundance is a social relationship, based on the principle that the means of one's existence will never be at stake in any of one's relationships. The steadfast security that such a principle implies is what allows all people to ask "What am I going to do with the time I am alive?" rather than "How am I going to keep living?"[24] Some will choose to follow a single idea to its end, others to periodically reinvent themselves. The main choice people will have to make is how to "balance the goal of bettering oneself against the injunction to better humanity" (as Captain Picard of the starship *Enterprise* tells a financial mogul, who had been cryogenically frozen in the twenty-first century only to be revived, to his horror, in a post-scarcity world).[25]

In such a world, there could still be sanctions to ensure that necessary work is actually undertaken. However, inducements to work would not take the form of threats of starvation, but invitations to cooperate. Economists have long recognized that hunger and homelessness are not the best motivators. Even in Kropotkin's time, economists admitted that "the best situation for man is when he produces in freedom, has choice in his occupations, has no overseer to impede him, and when he sees his work bring a profit to himself and others like him."[26] A bestselling writer on motivation recently rediscovered these same ideas: feelings of autonomy, mastery, and purpose are what generate the best work, not higher levels of monetary reward.[27]

The successful organization of a post-scarcity world would require that its denizens solve, to their satisfaction, the problems posed by the twentieth century's socialist calculation debates. They would do so with the tools of the twenty-first century: utilizing digital technologies to coordinate their needs and activities by designing

algorithms—which process data and present alternatives—and
protocols—which structure decisions about alternatives—that could
be further modified and adapted over time in light of experience.
Individuals would have to be able to use digital applications to articulate their needs and to transmit these to associations, while associations, in turn, would need to be able both to allocate resources among
themselves and to figure out how to make do with the resources they
are able to acquire, in a way that was fair and rational. Efficiency
would no longer be an overriding goal of production, but producers
would still have to be able to make reasonable choices among
production techniques, based on the ease with which they can access
different sorts of supplies. It would have to be possible, as well, to
hold producers accountable were they to fail to meet democratically
determined social standards. Again, there is likely to be no single best
way to deal with these crucial problems.[28]

Free Time for Everyone

For theorists of post-scarcity, the reconstruction of the realm of
necessity is not an end in itself; the solidarity it engenders also
expands the realm of freedom and ensures that this too is shared by
all.[29] Once necessity is assured, everyone is free to develop their individuality, outside the bounds of any given community. The point is to
enable by way of a collective social project what the automation theorists hope to achieve technologically, although advanced technologies will certainly play a role in expanding freedom's purview. Of
course, the realm of freedom is about having time for both socializing
and solitude, for engaging in hobbies and doing nothing at all—"*rien
faire comme une bête*, lying on water and looking peacefully at the
sky."[30] Frankfurt School critical theorist Theodor Adorno's phrase is
suggestive of a world in which material dispossession and the existential insecurity to which it gives rise have been universally abolished.
None of this requires that we assume a spontaneous harmony of
interests, or a benign human nature. On the contrary, an end to
economic compulsions implies that many people will be free to

withdraw from oppressive personal relationships within households or workplaces, or to renegotiate the terms of those engagements.[31]

What will people do with their expanded free time? Post-scarcity has been called "post-work," but such framing is inadequate.[32] After a period of rest and recovery, even the most work-weary people become restless and look for something to do. The reorganization of social life to reduce the role of necessary labor is not, therefore, about overcoming work as such; it is about freeing people to pursue activities that cannot be described simply as either work or leisure. That might include painting murals, learning languages, building waterslides—or discovering new ways to do common tasks to make them less time-consuming. It could mean writing novels, or self-reinvention through education or exploration. As automation theorists of both right and left envisage, the end of scarcity would enable people to enter voluntary associations with others from all over the globe: to join consortia of mathematical researchers, clubs for inventing new musical instruments, or federations for building spaceships. For most people, this would be the first time in their lives that they could enter truly voluntary agreements—without the gun to their heads of a pervasive material insecurity.

Under these conditions, "creative minds and scientific aptitudes" would no longer be "wasted due to accidents of birthplace, the bad luck of challenging circumstances, or the necessity to survive."[33] Funding for research or art would also no longer be determined by the profit motive, or dictated by the interests of the wealthy. What we call "capital" in the society of scarcity would, in post-scarcity, be recognized for what it is: *our common social inheritance*.[34] Built up over generations, belonging to no one and to everyone, it is that without which no one could achieve their larger goals, or even imagine them.

How would people gain access to the resources they need to pursue their passions? Presumably, many of these would be best developed within the realm of freedom itself, through voluntary associations and federation among them. At first, one might imagine the realm of necessity to be the one most like a capitalist economy, with its

attendant pressures to raise productivity, reduce labor time, and real-
locate resources. However, in the absence of market compulsions, it is
more likely that the realm of necessity would change slowly, by adapt-
ing innovations from the realm of freedom. The practical implementation of those innovations might take a long time, since the rush to
implement changes in process would no longer be enforced by market
competition, but instead would need to be decided through coordination among various committees—some of which might be more
concerned with simply getting their work done than with doing it
better. There would be no built-in growth trajectory, no need to grow
for growth's sake, especially given that most labors of necessity would
be services whose productivity is difficult to raise without sacrificing
quality.

In that case, the realm of freedom would be the one giving rise to
all manner of dynamism: that is where human beings would invent
new tools, instruments, and methods of accounting, as well as new
games and gadgets, rapidly reallocating resources over time and space
to suit changing human tastes. Since within the realm of freedom,
participation in any given association would be voluntary, no one
would need to keep doing what they had been doing on the sole basis
of survival. People would do only what they wanted to do.

The world would then be composed of overlapping partial plans,
which interrelate necessary and free activities, rather than a single
central plan. But these issues, as well as the related question of what
counts as necessity and what as freedom, would be matters for a freed
humanity to resolve for itself, politically. Within this framework, one
could imagine fully capacitated individuals arranging themselves in
all sorts of ways: people might live in large communities or small
ones; they might do a lot of work or a little, choosing instead to
explore nature, society, their minds, the oceans, or the stars; they
might be happy on a hot planet or a cool one, or in a world of relative
resource scarcity or abundance, as long as certain fundamental conditions of sustainable material security were met. The first thing people
would actually do in a post-scarcity world—alongside insuring everyone's basic needs were met—would be to put a large portion of

humanity's collective resources and intelligence to work to mitigate or reverse climate change, and to make up for the centuries of inequity that followed colonization.[35]

The point of this exercise is to show that it is possible to design utopian thought experiments that revolve around and prioritize people, rather than technological progress. Recognition of the fundamental dignity of the 7 billion plus who make up humanity requires that we no longer agree to relegate some to a life of drudgery so that others may be free. It means we must share out the work that remains to be done in a technologically advanced society, so that everyone has the right and the power to decide what to do with their time.

This brief sketch of a post-scarcity world can perhaps serve as a benchmark to evaluate the various pathways that are supposed to get us to that place. From this standpoint, it is clear that nothing about our world's present organization will automatically lead there. Economic growth never frees us from the need to grow more. Life expectancies, education levels, and degrees of urbanization have risen dramatically over time, yet remain highly unequal in their respective distributions. Meanwhile, even in the richest countries, most people are so atomized, materially insecure, and alienated from their collective capacities that their horizons are stunted. If full automation can appear as both a dream and a nightmare, that is because it has no innate association with human dignity, and because it will not generate a post-scarcity world by itself. Nor will universal basic income. Perhaps if access to education and healthcare were dramatically widened, communities revitalized through cooperative sharing of the work necessary to their reproduction, industries partially socialized, and massive investment made in the transition from fossil fuel to renewable sources of energy—then, a basic income could form one part of a larger project aiming at human freedom.[36] But the path to a post-scarcity world could also take some other form entirely. Without a clear vision of this coming world, it is easy to get lost along the way.

Postscript: Agents of Change

I F NEITHER TECHNOLOGICAL ADVANCEMENT nor technocratic reform leads inevitably to a post-scarcity world, then it is only the pressure of social movements, pushing for a radical restructuring of social life, that can bring it about. One of the most disappointing aspects of the automation discourse is its tendency to underrate existing social struggles. In their 1985 article "A Capitalist Road to Communism?," Robert van der Veen and Philippe van Parijs supposed that as "rapid labour-saving technical change" combined with "constraints on economic growth," rational human action could "be relied upon to generate, sooner or later" forces that demand and implement social change. Writing thirty years later, Nick Srnicek and Alex Williams despair of the forces that have been generated, which they describe as mere "folk politics": people are reacting to the increasing complexity of the modern world, they say, by demanding a return to the simplicity of local communities and engagement in face-to-face interactions.[1]

To despair of the emancipatory potential of today's social struggles is not unreasonable. It would take a massive and persistent mobilization to turn the tide of a truculent neoliberalism, yet the only movement with the size and strength to undertake this task—the historic labor movement—has been thoroughly defeated. Today, strikes and labor demonstrations are mainly defensive: workers fight to slow the pace of capital's juggernaut and its drive for more austerity, labor flexibility, and privatization, in response to an economic slowdown that never ends, but does get worse. The labor movement has never figured out how to respond to technologically induced job loss under conditions of slowing economic growth. As economic sociologist Wolfgang Streeck put it, "disorganized capitalism is disorganizing not only itself but its opposition as well."[2] For this reason, the long descent into economic stagnation has not been accompanied by a renewal of mass working-class organizations.

Nevertheless, in the years since the 2008 crisis, this political stasis has shown signs of cracking. Social struggles have unfolded on a scale not seen for decades. There have been waves of strikes and social movements across six continents—from China and Hong Kong to Algeria, Iraq, and Lebanon, from Argentina and Chile to France and Greece, and from Australia and Indonesia to the United States—with mass protests erupting again, worldwide, in 2019.[3] Masses of people have once again joined work stoppages, occupations, blockades, riots, and demonstrations, protesting against the symptoms of a long-term decline in the demand for labor, including rising inequality, employment insecurity, government corruption, and austerity measures, as well as food, energy, and transportation price hikes. Protestors have come out en masse in response to murders at the hands of the police, which sparked the rage of racialized communities who would no longer stand for their lack of social recognition.

To be sure, these explosive movements have so far lacked the staying power to force recalcitrant governments into retreat, and they have suffered reversals and defeats. But they have nevertheless broadened political horizons and radicalized a new generation of militants. Perhaps our era is like the mid nineteenth century not only because it has produced utopian visionaries, but also because it has generated new constituencies for emancipatory social change. Objective features of the past decade support this hypothesis: ours has been the most broadly educated, most urban and most connected population in world history. As journalist Paul Mason notes, literate and mobile people "will not accept a future of high inequality and stagnant growth" on a planet with rising sea levels.[4] Whether this will bring us closer to a freer future is an open question.

In early 2020, the spread of the COVID-19 pandemic temporarily halted the globalization of social struggles, but, with the simultaneous onset of a deep global recession, they are now beginning to resurge. What is certain is that, if these social movements take hold as more permanent formations, they are unlikely to look like the labor movements of earlier centuries. Vast discontinuities separate our era from theirs. Those labor movements arose during a long period of industrialization, whereas we live in the postindustrial doldrums: ours will be a struggle over the consequences of industrialization's end. This is not to deny the global economy's continuing dependence on industrial production, or the ongoing existence of factory workers. But the declining share of manufacturing in total employment means that these workers no longer have the capacity to cast themselves as representatives of a more just and rational future order. Even countries like South Africa, South Korea, and Brazil—which industrialized only recently, and where manufacturing workers were pivotal in the struggles for democracy of the 1970s and '80s—have long become majority service-sector economies.[5]

This change in the composition of the labor force will reshape social movements today in essential respects. Though the automation discourse tends to overemphasize this trend, it is true that direct human labor plays a much smaller role in the core industries than it did before; as Marx predicted, it has largely been displaced as the primary productive force by scientific and technical knowledge, embodied in vast infrastructures that mobilize both natural forces and machines. Many workers have been cast aside, forced to give up much of their waking lives to dead-end service jobs in which labor productivity rises slowly. Therefore, the dynamic struggles that animated earlier generations of workers—those concerning who should benefit from continual productivity growth—fail to take place. For most workers today, capital's compulsion to drive down production costs means only that labor intensifies, without corresponding increases in pay, which does not mean that workplace struggles are not occurring. It is only to say that their determining logics have evidently changed.

Some left commentators have argued that however disaffected insecure workers become, they lack the power at the point of production necessary to press their demands.[6] Yet, as it turns out, in a world of lean, just-in-time production, organizing to blockade circulation in and around major cities can prove an effective tactic. An early example is the *piquetero* movement in Argentina: beginning in the mid 1990s, unemployed workers blockaded highways around Buenos Aires to demand better benefits.[7] Since 2011, this tactic has been adopted sporadically by workers in the United States, France, Egypt, and elsewhere.

In the autonomous spaces that open up in the course of major struggles, movement participants pose questions about the nature and future of society. Assemblies are generally open to all. If personal and intimate forms of coercion are not altogether absent, there is nevertheless a shared sense that everyone deserves a say in social affairs. Within occupations and on the frontlines of blockades, people do actually care for one another. They cook and clean and look after the children without expecting anything in return, although they have, of course, generally purchased the materials they use to perform these tasks within the ordinary course of the life they seek to disrupt by such actions. These efforts do not merely indicate a penchant for a simpler life—whether in folk or *völkish* terms. Instead they point, however fitfully, toward a world of generalized human dignity, one with fewer borders and boundaries.

No matter how large they become, these protests have so far been unable to escape the limits confronted by all struggles over the collective reproduction of the working class, whose deterioration, under the pressures of stagnating wages, employment insecurity, and welfare-state retreat, has been extreme. These movements fail to rise from the level of *reproduction* to that of *production*, even when they call forth and combine with strikes in what remains of the industrial core. However much hope they inspire amid the catastrophe of the present, the 2020 COVID-19 pandemic notwithstanding, disruptive protests in our era have so far lacked a vision of a wholly different world: in which the infrastructures of capitalist societies are brought under collective control, work is reorganized and redistributed, scarcity is overcome through the free giving of goods and services, and our human capacities are correspondingly enlarged as new vistas of existential security and freedom open up.

Unless social struggles organize themselves around this historic task, the conquest of production, they will not break through to a new synthesis of what it means to be a human being—to live in a world devoid of poverty and billionaires, of stateless refugees and detention camps, and of lives spent in drudgery, which hardly offer a moment to rest, let alone dream. Movements without a vision are blind; but visionaries without movements are much more severely incapacitated. Without a massive social struggle to build a post-scarcity world, late-capitalist visionaries will remain mere techno-utopian mystics.

Notes

Chapter 1. The Automation Discourse

1 See Edward Bellamy's utopia, *Looking Backward, 2000–1887*, Oxford, 2007 [1888], p. 68.

2 See, respectively, Daniela Hernandez, "How to Survive a Robot Apocalypse: Just Close the Door," *Wall Street Journal*, November 10, 2017; David Autor, "Why Are There Still So Many Jobs? The History and Future of Workplace Automation," *Journal of Economic Perspectives*, vol. 29, no. 3, 2015, pp. 25–6.

3 Andy Puzder, "The Minimum Wage Should Be Called the Robot Employment Act," *Wall Street Journal*, April 3, 2017; Françoise Carré and Chris Tilly, *Where Bad Jobs Are Better: Retail Jobs across Countries and Companies*, Russell Sage, 2017.

4 This position is distinct from that of techno-optimists, like Ray Kurzweil, who imagine that technological change will generate a utopian world by itself, without the need for social transformation.

5 Erik Brynjolfsson and Andrew McAfee, *The Second Machine Age: Work, Progress, and Prosperity in a Time of Brilliant Technologies*, W.W. Norton, 2014, pp. 34, 128, 134ff, 172, 232.

6 Martin Ford, *Rise of the Robots: Technology and the Threat of a Jobless Future*, Basic Books, 2015, pp. xvii, 219.

7 See ibid., pp. 257–61. Among the many books coming out each year on the topic of automation, two recent titles stand out: Carl Benedikt Frey, *The Technology Trap: Capital, Labor, and Power in the Age of Automation*, Princeton, 2019; and Daniel Susskind, *A World without Work: Technology, Automation, and How We Should Respond*, Metropolitan, 2020. Arriving late in the wave of automation thinking, these books represent a pessimistic turn within the automation discourse. Frey does not think automation will necessarily generate a world without work, while Susskind does but disputes the viability of UBI as a solution.

8 Andy Kessler, "Zuckerberg's Opiate for the Masses," *Wall Street Journal*, June 18, 2017.

9 See, for example, Iain M. Banks, *Look to Windward*, Pocket Books, 2000; as well as his "Notes on the Culture," collected in Banks, *State of the Art*, Night Shade Books, 2004.

10 See, respectively, Claire Cain Miller, "A Darker Theme in Obama's Farewell: Automation Can Divide Us," *New York Times*, January 12, 2017; Kessler, "Zuckerberg's Opiate For the Masses"; Eduardo Porter, "Jobs Threatened by Machines: A Once 'Stupid' Concern Gains Respect," *New York Times*, June 7, 2016; Kevin Roose, "His 2020 Campaign Message: The Robots Are Coming," *New York Times*, February 12, 2018; Andrew Yang, *The War on Normal People: The Truth about America's Disappearing Jobs and Why Universal Basic Income Is Our Future*, Hachette, 2018; Andy Stern, *Raising the Floor: How a Universal Basic Income Can Renew Our Economy and Rebuild the American Dream*, PublicAffairs, 2016.

11 Nick Srnicek and Alex Williams, *Inventing the Future: Postcapitalism and a World without Work*, Verso, 2015, p. 112.

12 Peter Frase, *Four Futures: Life after Capitalism*, Verso, 2016; Manu Saadia, *Trekonomics: The Economics of Star Trek*, Inkshares, 2016.

13 Srnicek and Williams, *Inventing the Future*, p. 127.

14 Aaron Bastani, *Fully Automated Luxury Communism: A Manifesto*, Verso, 2019.

15 Martin Ford argues that the pandemic will "change consumer preference and really open up new opportunities for automation," as quoted in Zoe Thomas, "Coronavirus: Will Covid-19 speed up the use of robots to replace human workers?," *BBC News*, April 19, 2020. See also Michael Corkery and David Gelles, "Robots Welcome to Take Over, as Pandemic Accelerates Automation," *New York Times*, April 20, 2020; Carl Benedikt Frey, "Covid-19 will only increase automation anxiety," *Financial Times*, April 21, 2020. For a counterpoint, see Matt Simon, "If Robots Steal So Many Jobs, Why Aren't They Saving Us Now?," *Wired Magazine*, March 23, 2020.

16 Kurt Vonnegut, *Player Piano*, Dial Press, 2006 [1952], p. 73.

17 Carl Frey and Michael Osborne originally released their study as an Oxford Martin working paper online in 2013; it was later published as "The Future of Employment: How Susceptible Are Jobs to Computerization?," *Technological Forecasting and Social Change*, vol. 114, January 2017; Ljubica Nedelkoska and Glenda Quintini, "Automation, Skills Use, and Training," *OECD Social, Employment, and Migration Working Papers*, no. 202, 2018.

18 Quoted in Jerry Kaplan, "Don't Fear the Robots," *Wall Street Journal*, July 21, 2017. See Robert Atkinson and John Wu, "False Alarmism: Technological Disruption and the US Labor Market, 1850–2015," Information Technology and Innovation Foundation, 2017, itif.org.

19 Wassily Leontief, "Technological Advance, Economic Growth, and the Distribution of Income," *Population and Development Review*, vol. 9, no. 3, 1983, p. 404.

20 Keynes had a similar reaction to his own discovery that no mechanism in capitalist economies automatically generates full employment. See his "Economic Possibilities for Our Grandchildren (1930)," in *Essays in Persuasion*, Harcourt Brace, 1932; and William Beveridge, *Full Employment in a Free Society*, George Allen & Unwin, 1944, esp. pp. 21–3.

21 Karl Marx, *Capital: A Critique of Political Economy*, vol. 1, Penguin Classics, 1976 [1867], pp. 492–508.

22 Amy Sue Bix, *Inventing Ourselves out of Jobs: America's Debate over Technological Unemployment, 1929–1981*, Johns Hopkins University Press, 2000, pp. 305–7. See also Jason Smith, "Nowhere to Go: Automation, Then and Now," *Brooklyn Rail*, March–April 2017.

23 Two, more sinister, theories of a persistent labor underdemand have also periodically recurred in modern history: commentators have sometimes looked to Malthusian population dynamics for an explanation, and other times they have turned to spurious evidence that Jewish bankers are manipulating the money supply. See Ian Angus and Simon Butler, *Too Many People? Population, Immigration, and the Environmental Crisis*, Haymarket, 2011; Moishe Postone, "Anti-Semitism and National Socialism: Notes on the German Reaction to *Holocaust*," *New German Critique*, 19, S1, 1980.

24 See, for example, Jeanna Smialek and Keith Collins, "How the Fed Lost Its Faith in 'Full Employment,'" *New York Times*, December 12, 2019. Within the Fed system itself, R. Jason Faberman et. al. explain their view that since the 2008 crisis, "the unemployment rate" had captured "only a fraction of the potential slack in the labor market" due to the existence of discouraged workers, workers underemployed in terms of time, and workers underemployed in terms of wage-earning potentials. "The Shadow Margins of Labor Market Slack," NBER Working Paper 26852, March 2020. Of course, the COVID-19 pandemic recession rendered many of these debates moot.

25 Aaron Benanav, "Crisis and Recovery," *Phenomenal World*, April 3, 2020, available at phenomenalworld.org.

26 Global measures of the labor share include income from self-employment since many people in lower-income countries are own-account workers or unpaid family laborers.

27 See Josh Bivens and Lawrence Mishel, "Understanding the Historic Divergence between Productivity and a Typical Worker's Pay," EPI Briefing Paper 406, September 2015; Paolo Pasimeni, "The Relation between Productivity and

Compensation in Europe," European Commission Discussion Paper 79, March 2018.

28 See Kathleen Thelen, *Varieties of Liberalization and the New Politics of Social Solidarity*, Cambridge University Press, 2014.

29 See David Autor, "Paradox of Abundance: Automation Anxiety Returns," in Subramanian Rangan, ed., *Performance and Progress: Essays on Capitalism, Business, and Society*, Oxford University Press, 2015, p. 257; Robert J. Gordon, *Rise and Fall of American Growth*, Princeton University Press, 2016, p. 604.

30 See Fredric Jameson, *Archaeologies of the Future: The Desire Called Utopia and Other Science Fictions*, Verso, 2005.

31 James Boggs, "Manifesto for a Black Revolutionary Party," in Stephen M. Ward, ed., *Pages from a Black Radical's Notebook: A James Boggs Reader*, Wayne State University Press, 2011, p. 219.

Chapter 2. *Labor's Global Deindustrialization*

1 Estimated from ILO, *Key Indicators of the Labour Market*, 9th ed., 2015, which included projections for 2019. Within the global economy, many of these service workers are employed informally, picking through trash or selling food out of pushcarts, in jobs that could already have been eliminated with twentieth-century technologies: supermarkets, big-box retailers, refrigerated trucking, and so on.

2 Nick Dyer-Witheford, *Cyber-proletariat: Global Labour in the Digital Vortex*, Pluto, 2015, p. 184. Routine intellectual activities, even highly skilled ones, are apparently proving easier to automate than nonroutine manual jobs, which require more dexterity than machines presently possess. Erik Brynjolfsson and Andrew McAfee, *The Second Machine Age: Work, Progress, and Prosperity in a Time of Brilliant Technologies*, W.W. Norton, 2014, pp. 28–9.

3 Eve Batey, "Is SF Facing a Robot Food Apocalypse?," *Eater San Francisco*, January 8, 2020. See also Tim Carman, "This Automated Restaurant Was Supposed to Be the Future of Dining.

Until Humanity Struck Back," *Washington Post*, October 24, 2017.

4 See, for example, Brynjolfsson and McAfee, *Second Machine Age*, pp. 30–1; Martin Ford, *Rise of the Robots: Technology and the Threat of a Jobless Future*, Basic Books, 2015, pp. 1–12.

5 David Autor, "Why Are There Still So Many Jobs? The History and Future of Workplace Automation," *Journal of Economic Perspectives*, vol. 29, no. 3, 2015, p. 23.

6 Eileen Appelbaum and Ronald Schettkat, "Employment and Productivity in Industrialized Economies," *International Labour Review*, vol. 134, nos. 4–5, 1995, pp. 607–9.

7 Unless otherwise noted, statistics in the rest of this section are drawn from Conference Board, *International Comparisons of Manufacturing Productivity and Unit Labour Cost*, last updated January 2020, and *Total Economy Database*, last updated April 2019.

8 Fionna Tregenna, "Characterizing Deindustrialization: An Analysis of Changes in Manufacturing Employment and Output Internationally," *Cambridge Journal of Economics*, vol. 33, no. 3, 2009, p. 433.

9 Manufacturing is part of the larger industrial sector, which typically includes mining, construction, and utilities, and which has also seen declining employment shares, mostly but not exclusively due to job loss in manufacturing.

10 In the scholarly literature, see, for example, Robert Rowthorn and Ramana Ramaswamy's oft-cited paper, "Deindustrialization: Causes and Implications," IMF Working Paper 97/42, 1997. In the press, see Eduardo Porter, "Is the Populist Revolt Over? Not if Robots Have Their Way," *New York Times*, January 30, 2018.

11 Quoted in Brynjolfsson and McAfee, *Second Machine Age*, p. 100.

12 Ibid., pp. 43–5.

13 See Martin Neil Baily and Barry P. Bosworth, "US Manufacturing: Understanding Its Past and Its Potential Future," *Journal of Economic Perspectives*, vol. 28, no. 1, 2014; Daron Acemoglu et

al., "Return of the Solow Paradox? IT, Productivity, and Employment in US Manufacturing," *American Economic Review*, vol. 104, no. 5, 2014; and Susan Houseman, "Understanding the Decline of US Manufacturing Employment," Upjohn Institute Working Paper 18-287, 2018.

14 Baily and Bosworth, "US Manufacturing," p. 9. Computers and electronics count for 10 to 15 percent of US manufacturing output.

15 Daniel Michaels, "Foreign Robots Invade American Factory Floors," *Wall Street Journal*, March 26, 2017.

16 The countries with the highest levels of installed industrial robots per 10,000 manufacturing employees in 2016 included South Korea (631), Singapore (488), Germany (309), and Japan (303), as compared to the United States (189) and China (68), according to the International Federation of Robotics, "Robot Density Rises Globally," *IFR Press Releases*, February 7, 2018.

17 In standard economic accounting, value added is equivalent to the income earned in wages and profits after other intermediate costs have been deducted from total revenue.

18 This equation excludes the so-called small term, $\Delta P \Delta E$, as insignificant. Note that because this equation is true according to the very definition of labor productivity (O/E), it cannot be used to establish causality.

19 It is worth noting that job loss has been somewhat more severe in France compared to other European countries.

20 José Gabriel Palma, "Four Sources of 'Deindustrialization' and a New Concept of the 'Dutch Disease,'" in José Antonio Ocampo, ed., *Beyond Reforms: Structural Dynamics and Macroeconomic Vulnerability*, Stanford University Press, 2005, pp. 79–81. See Rowthorn and Ramaswamy, "Deindustrialization," p. 6, as well as Dani Rodrik, "Premature Deindustrialization," *Journal of Economic Growth*, vol. 21, no. 1, 2016, p. 7.

21 Rowthorn and Ramaswamy, "Deindustrialization," p. 20. See also Robert Rowthorn and Ken Coutts, "De-industrialisation and the balance of payments in advanced economies," *Cambridge Journal*

of Economics, vol. 28, no. 5, 2004. Although Rowthorn and his associates explained deindustrialization primarily in terms of differences between productivity growth rates in manufacturing and in services, they turned to a theory of evolutionary changes in the composition of demand to explain the existence of a prior period of industrialization, as well as to explain the timing of the turning point at which industrialization gave way to deindustrialization.

22 For example, deindustrialization—as measured by the fall in the manufacturing share of employment—started in Brazil in 1986, when the country's GDP per capita was $12,100 (measured in 2017 US dollars at purchasing power parity), that is, a little more than half of the GDP per capita of France at the time it began to deindustrialize, in 1973. South Africa, Indonesia, and Egypt had lower income levels at the time when their economies began to deindustrialize. See Sukti Dasgupta and Ajit Singh, "Manufacturing, Services, and Premature Deindustrialization in Developing Countries: A Kaldorian Analysis," in George Mavrotas and Anthony Shorrocks, eds., *Advancing Development: Core Themes in Global Economics*, Palgrave Macmillan, 2007; Tregenna, "Characterizing Deindustrialization."

23 Fiona Tregenna describes this process as "pre-industrialization deindustrialization" in "Deindustrialization, Structural Change, and Sustainable Economic Growth," UNIDO/UNU-MERIT Background Paper 32, 2015.

24 United Nations Industrial Development Organization, *Industrial Development Report 2018*, 2017, p. 166. UNIDO suggests that the global manufacturing share fell from 14.4 percent to 11.1 percent in the twenty-five years from 1991 to 2016. However, other sources put the mid-2010s share closer to 17 percent. The UNIDO numbers appear to be lower than other sources because of the stricter way they count employment in China's manufacturing sector.

25 Between 1993 and 2004, employment in state-owned enterprises declined by 40 percent, due to economic restructuring. See Barry

Naughton, *The Chinese Economy: Transitions and Growth*, MIT University Press, 2007, p. 105.

26 World Trade Organization, *International Trade Statistics 2015*, 2015. The data provided in table A1 is unique in that it stretches all the way back to the 1950s and covers total world production and exports for agriculture, mining, manufacturing, and economy as a whole. Unfortunately, the WTO stopped updating this data in 2015.

27 The World Bank has noted that since the global financial crisis, "trade has been growing more slowly not only because economic growth has become less trade-intensive, but also because global growth is slower." See Mary Hallward-Driemeier and Gaurav Nayyar, *Trouble in the Making? The Future of Manufacturing-Led Development*, World Bank, 2018, p. 81.

28 Robert Brenner has made this argument in *The Economics of Global Turbulence*, Verso, 2006, as well as in other works. Here, I am extending his account in order to explain labor deindustrialization. See also the related literature on the "fallacy of composition" in global trade, for example, Robert A. Blecker, "The Diminishing Returns to Export-Led Growth," a paper from the Project on Development, Trade, and International Finance, New York, 2000.

29 See Barry Eichengreen, *The European Economy Since 1945*, Princeton University Press, 2007, p. 18.

30 On US reorientation in the context of the Cold War, see ibid., pp. 54–8; Brenner, *Economics of Global Turbulence*, pp. 47–50; Yutaka Kosai, *The Era of High-Speed Growth*, University of Tokyo Press, 1986, pp. 53–68; and Herbert Giersch et al., *The Fading Miracle: Four Decades of Market Economy in Germany*, Cambridge University Press, 1992, pp. 17–26.

31 See Brenner, *Economics of Global Turbulence*, pp. 67–93. Eichengreen also describes "Europe after World War II" as a "classic example of export-led growth"; see *European Economy*, p. 38, and, on the role of technology transfers in particular, pp. 24–6. On the role of the 1949 devaluations, see pp. 77–9, and Kosai,

High-Speed Growth, pp. 67–8. See also Nixon Apple, "The Rise and Fall of Full Employment Capitalism," *Studies in Political Economy*, vol. 4, no. 1, 1980.

32 See Brenner, *Economics of Global Turbulence*, pp. 50–1, 122–42. Since the 1970s, whether a given region rushed ahead or fell behind, economically, depended largely on the whiplashing of international currency valuations: the dollar's value fell from 1971 to 1979, rose from 1979 to 1985, fell again from 1985 to 1995, rose thereafter, and so on—in each period pulling dollar-denominated currencies up and down with it, with ramifications for international competitiveness. This seesawing makes it impossible to evaluate world market trends on the basis of patterns prevailing in the US alone, a tendency that remains all too common in the economics literature.

33 See UNCTAD, *Trade and Development Report 2006*, 2006, pp. 42–50; Kiminori Matsuyama, "Structural Change in an Interdependent World: A Global View of Manufacturing Decline," *Journal of the European Economic Association*, vol. 7, nos. 2–3, 2009, pp. 478–86.

34 For a helpful summary of this argument, see Robert Brenner interviewed by Jeong Seong-jin, "Overproduction Not Financial Collapse is the Heart of the Crisis: The US, East Asia and the World," *Asia-Pacific Journal*, vol. 7, issue 6, no. 5, 2009.

35 See Brenner, *Economics of Global Turbulence*, pp. 108–14. For a graphic representation, see UNIDO, *Industrial Development Report 2018*, p. 172. It is important to note that differences between manufacturing and nonmanufacturing price trends can also be explained to some extent by Baumol's cost disease.

36 See Rodrik, "Premature Deindustrialization," p. 4.

37 See Brenner, *Economics of Global Turbulence*, pp. 37–40. The decline in the demand for investment goods in turn depressed overall demand. The result was that what looked like worsening overproduction from one perspective appeared, from another, as worsening underinvestment and hence underdemand, which resulted in slower rates of market growth and fiercer competition.

38 All firms, regardless of whether they use advanced technologies, must consistently upgrade their capacities. See Sanjaya Lall, "The Technological Structure and Performance of Developing Country Manufactured Exports, 1985–98," *Oxford Development Studies*, vol. 28, no. 3, 2000, pp. 337–69.

39 In poorer countries where the labor force is growing rapidly, the decline in manufacturing employment growth is typically relative rather than absolute. The manufacturing employment share declines even as its level grows.

40 See Gary Gereffi, "The Organization of Buyer-Driven Global Commodity Chains: How US Retailers Shape Overseas Production Networks," in Gary Gereffi and Miguel Korzeniewics, eds., *Commodity Chains and Global Capitalism*, Praeger, 1994. For a more recent account, see William Milberg and Deborah Winkler, *Outsourcing Economics: Global Value Chains in Capitalist Development*, Cambridge University Press, 2013.

41 Brenner, *Economics of Global Turbulence*, p. 113.

42 For an early account of this process, see G.K. Helleiner, "Manufacturing Exports from Less-Developed Countries and Multinational Firms," *Economic Journal*, vol. 83, no. 329, 1973, p. 28ff. Between 1966 and 1980, US imports of goods produced in that country but then assembled abroad rose in value from $953 million to almost $14 billion, an increase of more than 1,300 percent in fifteen years. See US International Trade Commission, *Imports under Items 806.30 and 807.00 of the Tariff Schedules of the United States, 1984–87*, 1988.

43 Dyer-Witheford, *Cyber-Proletariat*, p. 71.

44 See Gary Herrigel, *Manufacturing Possibilities: Creative Action and Industrial Recomposition in the United States, Germany, and Japan*, Oxford University Press, 2010.

45 For an account of China's rust belt in a global comparative context, see Ching Kwan Lee, *Against the Law: Labour Struggles in China's Rustbelt and Sunbelt*, University of California Press, 2007, esp. pp. 242–58.

46 Peter Goodman, "The Robots Are Coming and Sweden Is Fine," *New York Times*, December 27, 2017; Yuri Kageyama, "Reverence for Robots: Japanese Workers Treasure Automation," *Associated Press News*, August 16, 2017. For robot density statistics, see International Federation of Robotics, "Robot Density Rises Globally."

47 Hallward-Driemeier and Nayyar, *Trouble in the Making?*, pp. 97–8.

Chapter 3. In the Shadow of Stagnation

1 Unless otherwise noted, MVA and GDP growth rates will be cited in real inflation-adjusted terms, rather than in nominal terms. Measures of GDP growth and labor productivity, the latter in terms of real value added per employee, derive from Conference Board, *Total Economy Database*, last updated November 2018.

2 In Germany, MVA and GDP growth rates have fallen since 1973, but MVA is still growing at a faster pace than GDP. Meanwhile, in Italy, the economy has completely stagnated.

3 See William Baumol, "Macroeconomics of Unbalanced Growth: The Anatomy of Urban Crisis," in *American Economic Review*, vol. 57, no. 3, June 1967, pp. 415–26; Robert Rowthorn and Ramana Ramaswamy, "Deindustrialization: Causes and Implications," IMF Working Paper 97/42, 1997, pp. 9–11; Dani Rodrik, "Premature Deindustrialization," *Journal of Economic Growth*, vol. 21, no. 1, 2016, p. 16.

4 Data on capital stock derives from the *Penn World Table 9.1*, last updated September 2019, retrieved from FRED, Federal Reserve Bank of St. Louis on May 9, 2020.

5 See Joseph Schumpeter, *Business Cycles*, vol. 1, McGraw-Hill, 1939, pp. 93–4.

6 Some economists have attempted to theorize tendential economic stagnation and its relationship to rising inequality. See, for example, Thomas Piketty, *Capital in the Twenty-First Century*,

Harvard University Press, 2014; Robert J. Gordon, *Rise and Fall of American Growth*, Princeton University Press, 2016; and the essays collected around Lawrence Summers's hypothesis in Coen Teulings and Richard Baldwin, eds., *Secular Stagnation: Facts, Causes, and Cures*, Vox, 2014.

7 For the original account of this phenomenon, see Nicholas Kaldor, *Causes of the Slow Rate of Economic Growth in the United Kingdom*, Cambridge University Press, 1966. For an extended discussion, see also Mary Hallward-Driemeier and Gaurav Nayyar, *Trouble in the Making? The Future of Manufacturing-Led Development*, World Bank, 2018, pp. 9–37.

8 See A.P. Thirlwall, "A Plain Man's Guide to Kaldor's Growth Laws," *Journal of Post-Keynesian Economics*, vol. 5, no. 3, 1983, pp. 345–6. For the technological exhaustion thesis, see Gordon, *Rise and Fall of American Growth*.

9 See Adam Szirmai, "Industrialization as an Engine of Growth in Developing Countries, 1950–2005," in *Structural Change and Economic Dynamics*, vol. 23, no. 4, 2012, pp. 406–20. See also Adam Szirmai and Bart Verspagen, "Manufacturing and Economic Growth in Developing Countries, 1950–2005," *Structural Change and Economic Dynamics*, vol. 34, September 2015, pp. 46–59.

10 Robert Scott, "The Manufacturing Footprint and the Importance of US Manufacturing Jobs," Economic Policy Institute Briefing Paper 388, January 22, 2015.

11 Gross manufacturing output shares for the United States taken from the United States Bureau of Economic Analysis and for Japan from Statistics Bureau of Japan, *Japan Statistical Yearbook 2020*, Table 3-5, "Gross Domestic Product and Factor Income Classified by Economic Activities (at Current Prices)," p. 100.

12 See Robert Brenner, "What's Good for Goldman Sachs Is Good for America," prologue to the Spanish translation of his *Economics of Global Turbulence*, Akal, 2009. For an alternative account, see Robert Skidelsky, *Keynes: The Return of the Master*, PublicAffairs, 2010.

13 See Robert Brenner, *The Boom and the Bubble: The US in the World Economy*, Verso, 2002, pp. 188–217.

14 See Rana Foroohar, "US Economy Is Dangerously Dependent on Wall Street Whims," *Financial Times*, March 8, 2020.

15 See John Plender, "Why 'Japanification' Looms for the Sluggish Eurozone," *Financial Times*, March 19, 2009. See also Richard Koo, *The Holy Grail of Macroeconomics: Lessons from Japan's Great Recession*, Wiley, 2008.

16 Brenner, *Economics of Global Turbulence*, pp. 153–7. See also Gary Herrigel, *Manufacturing Possibilities: Creative Action and Industrial Recomposition in the United States, Germany, and Japan*, Oxford University Press, 2010.

17 For the analysis that follows, see Brenner, *Boom and Bubble*, pp. 48–93.

18 See R. Taggart Murphy, *The Weight of the Yen*, W.W. Norton, 1996, pp. 165–94; Herbert Giersch et al., *The Fading Miracle: Four Decades of Market Economy in Germany*, Cambridge University Press, 1992, pp. 185–255; Brenner, *Boom and Bubble*, pp. 94–127.

19 Murphy, *Weight of the Yen*, pp. 195–218, 239–310; see also R. Taggart Murphy, *Japan and the Shackles of the Past*, Oxford University Press, 2014; Perry Anderson, "Situationism à l'Enverse?," *New Left Review* 119, S2, September–October 2019, pp. 74–7.

20 Brenner, *Boom and Bubble*, pp. 128–70.

21 Brenner, *Economics of Global Turbulence*, pp. 153–7.

22 Manufactures account for 70 percent of global trade; primary commodities, including agricultural goods, fuel, and minerals account for 25 percent; services account for just 5 percent. World Trade Organization, *World Trade Statistical Review 2018*, 2018, p. 11. On overproduction in agriculture, see UN Food and Agriculture Organization, *State of Food and Agriculture 2000*, 2000.

23 Between 2001 and 2007, global MVA growth rates rose to 3.5 percent per year. They then fell to 1.6 percent per year between

2008 and 2014. On convergence, see Michael Spence, *The Next Convergence: The Future of Economic Growth in a Multispeed World*, FSG, 2011; see also Dani Rodrik, "The Future of Economic Convergence," NBER Working Paper 17400, 2011.

24 Conference Board, *Total Economy Database*. See also Richard Freeman, "The Great Doubling: The Challenge of the New Global Labour Market," in J. Edwards et al., eds., *Ending Poverty in America: How to Restore the American Dream*, New Press, 2007.

25 See Mike Davis, *Planet of Slums*, Verso, 2006. See also Aaron Benanav, "Demography and Dispossession: Explaining the Growth of the Global Informal Workforce, 1950–2000," *Social Science History*, vol. 43, no. 4, 2019, pp. 679–703.

26 For example, from 1870 to 1913, GDP grew at an average rate of 1.9 percent per year in the UK (as compared to 1.6 percent per year for 2001–17), 1.6 percent per year in France (as compared to 1.2 percent per year), and 2.9 percent per year in Germany (as compared to 1.4 percent per year). See Stephen Broadberry and Kevin O'Rourke, *The Cambridge Economic History of Modern Europe*, vol. 2, *1870 to the Present*, Cambridge University Press, 2010, p. 36.

27 In 1913, 47 percent of Europe's population was still working in agriculture. Ibid., p. 61.

28 See Paul Bairoch, "International Industrialization Levels from 1750 to 1980," *Journal of European Economic History*, vol. 11, no. 2, Fall 1982. See also Jeffrey Williamson, *Trade and Poverty: When the Third World Fell Behind*, MIT Press, 2011.

29 See, for example, Alexander Keyssar, *Out of Work: The First Century of Unemployment in Massachussetts*, Cambridge University Press, 1986; Christian Topalov, *Naissance du chômeur, 1880–1919*, Albin Michel, 1994.

30 Kristin Ross draws an evocative parallel between the experiences of the workers who entered Occupy Oakland, on the one hand, and the Paris Commune, on the other, in *Communal Luxury: The Political Imaginary of the Paris Commune*, Verso, 2015, p. 3.

31　Óscar Jordá, Sanjay R. Singh, and Alan M. Taylor, "Longer-run Economic Consequences of Pandemics," NBER Working Paper 26934, 2020.

32　See Joseph Schumpeter, *Capitalism, Socialism, and Democracy*, Routledge, 2003, pp. 81–6.

33　Andy Stern, *Raising the Floor: How a Universal Basic Income Can Renew Our Economy and Rebuild the American Dream*, PublicAffairs, 2016, pp. 7–8. See also Andrew Yang, *The War on Normal People: The Truth about America's Disappearing Jobs and Why Universal Basic Income Is Our Future*, Hachette, 2018, p. 94.

34　See, for example, Ray Kurzweil, *The Singularity Is Near*, Viking, 2005, p. 67. For a critique, see Gordon, *Rise and Fall of American Growth*, pp. 444–7. Gordon argues that since 2005, Moore's law has collapsed. See also Tom Simonite, "Moore's Law is Dead. Now What?," *MIT Technology Review*, May 13, 2016.

35　For a set of critical reflections by AI scientists, who mostly doubt that general AI is anywhere near this level of development, see Martin Ford, *Architects of Intelligence: The Truth about AI from the People Building It*, Packt Publishing, 2018.

36　James Vincent, "Former Facebook Exec Says Social Media Is Ripping Apart Society," *Verge*, December 11, 2017; Mattha Busby, "Social Media Copies Gambling Methods 'to Create Psychological Cravings,'" *Guardian*, May 8, 2018.

37　See Raniero Panzieri, "The Capitalist Use of Machinery: Marx versus the Objectivists," in Phil Slater, ed., *Outlines of a Critique of Technology*, Humanities Press, 1980; Derek Sayer, *The Violence of Abstraction*, Basil Blackwell, 1987.

38　See Nick Dyer-Witheford, *Cyber-proletariat: Global Labour in the Digital Vortex*, Pluto, 2015, pp. 87–93.

39　For the classic account, see David Noble, *Forces of Production: A Social History of Industrial Automation*, Knopf, 1984. See also Tony Smith, *Technology and Capital in the Age of Lean Production: A Marxian Critique of the "New Economy,"* SUNY Press, 2000; and Gavin Mueller, *Breaking Things at Work: The Luddites Are Right about Why You Hate Your Job*, Verso, 2020.

40 Ceylan Yeginsu, "If Workers Slack Off, the Wristband Will Know. (And Amazon Has a Patent for It.)," *New York Times*, February 1, 2018; Beth Gutelius and Nik Theodore, *The Future of Warehouse Work: Technological Change in the US Logistics Industry*, UC Berkeley Center for Labor Research and Education, October 2019.

41 Strong tariff protections against imports were also key. See Niek Koning, *The Failure of Agrarian Capitalism: Agrarian Politics in the UK, Germany, the Netherlands, and the USA, 1846–1919*, Routledge, 2002.

42 See UN Food and Agriculture Organization, *State of Food and Agriculture 2000*; and Marcel Mazoyer and Laurence Roudart, *A History of World Agriculture: From the Neolithic Age to the Current Crisis*, Monthly Review, 2006, pp. 375–440.

43 Statistics drawn from Groningen Growth and Development Centre, *10-Sector Database*, updated January 2015; global agricultural employment share for the 1980s from David Grigg, "Agriculture in the World Economy: an Historical Geography of Decline," *Geography*, vol. 77, no. 3, 1992, p. 221 and for 2018 from ILO, *World Employment and Social Outlook – Trends 2019*, 2019, p. 14.

44 See Martin Ford, *Rise of the Robots: Technology and the Threat of a Jobless Future*, Basic Books, 2015, pp. 181–91; Stern, *Raising the Floor*, pp. 69–70. See also Conor Dougherty, "Self-Driving Trucks May Be Closer Than They Appear," *New York Times*, November 13, 2017. Robert Gordon, ever the skeptic, doubts the hype. See Gordon, *Rise and Fall of American Growth*, p. 599ff.

45 Although it employs fewer workers worldwide, the mining industry may be the first to widely deploy automated production. For Rio Tinto's plans in Western Australia, see William Wilkes, "How the World's Biggest Companies are Fine-Tuning the Robot Revolution," Dow Jones Institutional News, May 14, 2018.

46 See Ellen Israel Rosen, *Making Sweatshops: The Globalization of the US Apparel Industry*, University of California Press, 2002; and Jefferson Cowie, *Capital Moves: RCA's Seventy-Year Quest for Cheap Labour*, New Press, 1999.

47 Phil Neel, "Swoosh," *Ultra*, November 8, 2015, available at ultra-com.org; Anna Nicolaou and Kiran Stacey, "Stitched up by Robots," *Financial Times*, July 19, 2017; Jennifer Bissell-Linsk, "Robotics in the Running," *Financial Times*, October 23, 2017; Jon Emont, "The Robots Are Coming for Garment Workers. That's Good for the US, Bad for Poor Countries," *Wall Street Journal*, February 16, 2018; Kevin Sneader and Jonathan Woetzel, "China's Impending Robot Revolution," *Wall Street Journal*, August 3, 2016; Saheli Roy Choudhury, "China Wants to Build Robots to Overtake Its Rivals—But It's Not There Yet," CNBC, August 16, 2018; Brahima Coulibaly, "Africa's Race against the Machines," *Project Syndicate*, June 16, 2017; AFP, "Tech to Cost Southeast Asia Millions of Jobs, Doom 'Factory Model,' Warns WEF," *AFP International Text Wire*, September 12, 2018.

48 Hallward-Driemeier and Nayyar, *Trouble in the Making?*, pp. 93–6. Global employment in the IT and call center sectors also seems set to decline as cloud-based computing obviates the need for firms to develop and monitor their own websites and online databases; large Indian IT firms are already shedding jobs. See Simon Mundy, "India's Tech Workers Scramble for Jobs as Industry Automates," *Financial Times*, May 27, 2017.

49 Nathaniel Meyersohn, "Grocery Stores Turn to Robots during the Coronavirus," *CNN Business*, April 7, 2020. See also John Reed, Mercedes Ruehl, and Benjamin Parkin, "Coronavirus: will call centre workers lose their 'voice' to AI?," *Financial Times*, April 22, 2020.

Chapter 4. A Low Demand for Labor

1 Wassily Leontief, "Technological Advance, Economic Growth and the Distribution of Income," *Population and Development Review*, vol. 9, no. 3, 1983, p. 409; Erik Brynjolfsson and Andrew McAfee, *The Second Machine Age: Work, Progress, and Prosperity in a Time of Brilliant Technologies*, W.W. Norton, 2014, p. 179. Nick Dyer-Witheford speaks of a "deepening pool of

unemployed populations, no longer required by digital capital" (*Cyber-proletariat: Global Labour in the Digital Vortex*, Pluto, 2015, p. 3), while Andrew Yang refers to a "growing mass of the permanently displaced" (*The War on Normal People: The Truth about America's Disappearing Jobs and Why Universal Basic Income Is Our Future*, Hachette, 2018, p. xli).

2 According to science fiction writer Arthur C. Clarke, "the goal of the future is full unemployment, so we can play": "Free Press Interview: A. C. Clarke," *Los Angeles Free Press*, April 25, 1969. See also Brynjolfsson and McAfee, *Second Machine Age*, pp. 180–1; and Martin Ford, *Rise of the Robots: Technology and the Threat of a Jobless Future*, Basic Books, 2015, pp. 194–6.

3 On the limits of unemployment as a measure of labor market health, see David Blanchflower, *Not Working: Where Have All the Good Jobs Gone?*, Princeton University Press, 2019. On the genesis of unemployment as an economic category, see Michael Piore, "Historical Perspectives and the Interpretation of Unemployment," *Journal of Economic Literature*, vol. 25, no. 4, 1987.

4 Yang, *War on Normal People*, p. 80. Laura Tyson, "Labour Markets in the Age of Automation," *Project Syndicate*, June 7, 2017.

5 For an account of how different welfare-state regimes adapted to the return of high unemployment, see Gøsta Esping-Andersen, *Social Foundations of Postindustrial Economies*, Oxford University Press, 1999; Kathleen Thelen, *Varieties of Liberalization and the New Politics of Social Solidarity*, Cambridge University Press, 2014; and Lucio Baccaro and Chris Howell, *Trajectories of Neoliberal Transformation: European Industrial Relations since the 1970s*, Cambridge University Press, 2017. See also J. Timo Weishaupt, *From the Manpower Revolution to the Activation Paradigm: Explaining Institutional Continuity and Change in an Integrating Europe*, University of Amsterdam Press, 2011.

6 Exceptions to this trend include France, Spain, Austria, and Italy, which continue to spend significant amounts of money on

out-of-work income maintenance and support, and have higher average rates of unemployment.

7 OECD, *Measuring the Digital Transformation: A Roadmap for the Future*, 2019, p. 175. Sweden had adopted active labor market policies earlier in the postwar era; in later decades, other countries followed Sweden's lead.

8 Karl Marx, *Capital: A Critique of Political Economy*, vol. 1, Penguin Classics, 1976 [1867], pp. 796 and 798. For an extended analysis of how Marx's concept of the relative surplus population can be applied in our own times, see Aaron Benanav and John Clegg, "Crisis and Immiseration: Critical Theory Today," in Beverley Best, Werner Bonefeld, and Chris O'Kane, eds., *SAGE Handbook of Frankfurt School Critical Theory*, Sage, 2018, 1629–48; as well as Endnotes and Aaron Benanav, "Misery and Debt," *Endnotes*, no. 2, 2010; and Endnotes, "An Identical-Abject Subject," *Endnotes*, no. 4, 2015.

9 For a related comparative-institutional analysis, focused on the advanced capitalist countries, see Arne Kalleberg, *Precarious Lives: Job Insecurity and Well-Being in Rich Democracies*, Polity, 2018.

10 Josh Bivens and Lawrence Mishel, "Understanding the Historic Divergence between Productivity and a Typical Worker's Pay," EPI Briefing Paper 406, September 2015.

11 See Paul Beaudry et al., "The Great Reversal in the Demand for Skill and Cognitive Tasks," NBER Working Paper 18901, 2013; Elise Gould, "Higher Returns on Education Can't Explain Growing Wage Inequality," *Working Politics* (blog), Economics Policy Institute, March 15, 2019; Lawrence Mishel et. al., "Wage Stagnation in Nine Charts," EPI Report, January 6, 2015. For an extended critique of skill-biased technical change as an explanation of rising economic inequality, see John Schmitt, Heidi Shierholz, and Lawrence Mishel, "Don't Blame the Robots: Assessing the Job Polarization Explanation of Growing Wage Inequality," EPI–CEPR Working Paper, 2013.

12 For an analysis of the legal context of recent technological developments, which also casts doubt on the automation theorists'

account, see Brishen Rogers, "The Law and Political Economy of Workplace Technological Change," *Harvard Civil Rights-Civil Liberties Law Review*, vol. 55, 2020. See also Nick Srnicek, *Platform Capitalism*, Polity, 2016.

13 Bureau of Labor Statistics, *Contingent and Alternative Employment Relations*, May 2017.

14 Key exceptions are Sweden and, in the early postwar period, the UK, where labor market institutions were designed by Social Democratic and Labor governments. See Gøsta Esping-Andersen, *The Three Worlds of Welfare Capitalism*, Princeton University Press, 1990.

15 OECD, *Indicators of Employment Protection*, last updated 2014. These data provide measures of the procedures and costs of employee dismissal.

16 See Esping-Andersen, *Social Foundations*, pp. 107–11. See also Patrick Emmenegger et al., eds., *The Age of Dualization: The Changing Face of Inequality in Deindustrializing Societies*, Oxford University Press, 2012, on the evolution of insider/outsider distinctions within European welfare states.

17 For an analysis of deteriorating labor market conditions in Germany, see Oliver Nachtwey, *Germany's Hidden Crisis: Social Decline in the Heart of Europe*, Verso, 2018, esp. pp. 103–61.

18 See ILO, *Non-Standard Employment around the World*, 2016. See also Paolo Barbieri and Giorgio Cutuli, "Employment Protection Legislation, Labour Market Dualism, and Inequality in Europe," *European Sociological Review*, vol. 32, no. 4, 2016, pp. 501–16.

19 See Brett Neilson and Ned Rossiter, "Precarity as a Political Concept, or, Fordism as Exception," *Theory, Culture, and Society*, vol. 25, nos. 7–8, 2008.

20 See Bruno Palier and Kathleen Thelen, "Institutionalizing Dualism: Complementarities and Change in France and Germany," *Politics and Society*, vol. 38, no. 1, 2010; David Rueda, "Dualization, Crisis, and the Welfare State," *Socio-Economic Review*, vol. 12, no. 2, 2014.

21 OECD, *In It Together: Why Less Inequality Benefits All*, 2015, p. 144. See also Shiho Futagami, "Non-Standard Employment in Japan: Gender Dimensions," International Institute for Labour Studies Discussion Paper DP/200/2010, 2010, p. 29. See also Kalleberg, *Precarious Lives*, pp. 73–107.

22 OECD, *Economic Outlook*, 2018, p. 54.

23 See Aaron Benanav, "The Origins of Informality: The ILO at the Limit of the Concept of Unemployment," *Journal of Global History*, vol. 14, no. 1, 2019, pp. 107–25.

24 Jacques Charmes, "The Informal Economy Worldwide: Trends and Characteristics," *Margin: The Journal of Applied Economic Research*, vol. 6, no. 2, 2012, pp. 103–32. See also Aaron Benanav, "Demography and Dispossession: Explaining the Growth of the Global Informal Workforce, 1950–2000," *Social Science History*, vol. 43, no. 4, 2019.

25 Jan Breman and Marcel van der Linden, "Informalizing the Economy: The Return of the Social Question at a Global Level," *Development and Change*, vol. 45, no. 5, 2014.

26 See Pun Ngai, *Migrant Labor in China: Post-socialist Transformations*, Polity, 2016.

27 In sub-Saharan Africa, only 3 percent of workers are covered by unemployment benefits—as compared to 76 percent in high-income countries: ILO, *World Employment Social Outlook: The Changing Nature of Jobs*, 2015, p. 80.

28 See, respectively, the ILO's *Key Indicators*, and *Women and Men in the Informal Economy: A Statistical Picture*, 3rd ed., 2018, p. 23.

29 ILO, *World Employment Social Outlook*, p. 31.

30 See Ronaldo Munck, "The Precariat: A View from the South," *Third World Quarterly*, vol. 34, no. 5, 2013.

31 Some automation theorists do identify underemployment as a common feature of contemporary economies, but they have trouble explaining it, focused as they are on the apparent dynamism of technological change. See, for example, Andy Stern, *Raising the Floor: How a Universal Basic Income Can*

Renew Our Economy and Rebuild the American Dream, PublicAffairs, 2016, p. 185; and Yang, *War on Normal People*, pp. 79–80.

32 That was more or less the plot of *In Time* (2011), written and directed by Andrew Niccol. See also Alfonso Cuarón's *Children of Men* (2006), and Neill Blomkamp's *District 9* (2009) and *Elysium* (2013), as well as the Brazilian TV series *3%* (2016), created by Pedro Aguilera.

33 ILO, *Key Indicators*. Of that 17 percent, a sizable fraction are informally employed, engaging in domestic industry: the production of bricks, cigarettes, locks, and shoes in tiny household or backyard shops and foundries.

34 According to the ILO's *Key Indicators*, service workers came to represent the majority of the global labor force in 2020.

35 Daniel Bell, *The Coming of Post-industrial Society*, Basic Books, 1973.

36 See William Baumol, "Macroeconomics of Unbalanced Growth: The Anatomy of Urban Crisis," *American Economic Review*, vol. 57, no. 3, June 1967, pp. 415–26; as well as Baumol et al., *Productivity and American Leadership: The Long View*, MIT Press, 1989.

37 William Baumol et. al., "Unbalanced Growth Revisited: Asymptotic Stagnancy and New Evidence," *American Economics Review*, vol. 75, no. 4, 1985, p. 806.

38 For a similar analysis, see Servaas Storm, "The New Normal: Demand, Secular Stagnation, and the Vanishing Middle Class," *International Journal of Political Economy*, no. 46, 2017, pp. 169–210, although Storm claims that job shedding in the dynamic sectors of the economy is due to automation rather than to international overcapacity.

39 Jonathan Gershuny and I.D. Miles, *The New Service Economy*, Praeger, 1983, p. 22. See also Jonathan Gershuny, *After Industrial Society? The Emerging Self-Service Economy*, Macmillian, 1978, pp. 56–7.

40 See Baumol et. al., "Unbalanced Growth Revisited." Some service sub-sectors, like trade and transportation in the United States,

have seen more rapid productivity growth since the year 2000. However, innovations in this sub-sector have failed to generate sustained, sector-wide productivity growth of the sort that was endemic to manufacturing over the long history of its industrial development. Services like warehousing have typically been "asymptotically stagnant," in Baumol's language. They consist of separable components, some of which can be rendered more efficient via an industrial process and some of which (like stocking and picking items in warehouses) cannot. Over time, as the former tasks become more efficient, the latter come to predominate in terms of employment. Although asymptotic stagnation is generally a feature of services, it is found in some labor-intensive industries, such as apparel sewing and the electronics assembly, which have played a major role in generating manufacturing jobs worldwide and are now threatened by automation.

41 According to Baumol, it is actually the falling price of manufactures that makes services seem to grow more expensive. The theory that changes in relative prices are determined by differential rates of labor productivity growth was the original intuition behind the labor theory of value. See Adam Smith, *Wealth of Nations*, David Campbell Publishers, 2000 [1776], pp. 73–4.

42 For a similar explanation, see Torben Iversen and Anne Wren, "Equality, Employment, and Budgetary Restraint: The Trilemma of the Service Economy," *World Politics*, vol. 50, no. 4, 1998; see also Storm, "The New Normal."

43 OECD, *Employment Outlook*, 1987, pp. 10–11.

44 David Autor and Anna Salomons, "Is Automation Labour-Displacing? Productivity Growth, Employment, and the Labour Share," *Brookings Papers on Economic Activity*, 2018, pp. 2–3.

45 ILO and OECD, "The Labour Share in the G20 Economies," report prepared for the G20 Employment Working Group, February 2015, p. 3. IMF, *World Economic Outlook*, 2017, p. 3. See also Loukas Karabarbounis and Brent Neiman, "The Global Decline of the Labour Share," *Quarterly Journal of Economics*, vol. 129, no. 1, 2014.

46 Andrew Sharpe and James Uguccioni, "Decomposing the Productivity-Wage Nexus in Selected OECD Countries, 1986–2013," in *International Productivity Monitor*, no. 32, 2017, p. 31.

47 See Thomas Piketty, *Capital in the Twenty-First Century*, Harvard University Press, pp. 407–9, on the number of servants the top 1 percent of wealth inheritors can employ, compared to top labor-income earners.

48 Ford, *Rise of the Robots*, p. 219; Mike Davis, *Planet of Slums*, Verso, 2006, p. 199.

49 Some portion of the income gains of the poorest 50 percent was eaten up by higher living costs in cities, which are notoriously difficult to measure; urbanization increased from 39 to 54 percent over the same period.

50 Facundo Alvaredo et al., eds., *World Inequality Report 2018*, Harvard University Press, 2018, p. 52.

51 See the analysis of this global phenomenon in United Nations, *Human Development Report 2019: Beyond Income, beyond Averages, beyond Today: Inequalities in Human Development in the 21st Century*, 2019.

52 See Kalleberg, *Precarious Lives*, pp. 130–49; and Blanchflower, *Not Working*, pp. 212–37.

53 OECD, *Employment Outlook*, 2019, p. 29.

54 Marcel van der Linden, "The Crisis of World Labor," *Solidarity*, no. 176, May–June 2015.

Chapter 5. Silver Bullets?

1 These ideas are not limited to the right. See Jamie Merchant, "Fantasies of Secession: A Critique of Left Economic Nationalism," *Brooklyn Rail*, February 2018.

2 See, inter alia, Darrell West, *The Future of Work: Robots, AI, and Automation*, Brookings Institution Press, 2018, p. 139; Andrew Yang, *The War on Normal People: The Truth about America's Disappearing Jobs and Why Universal Basic Income Is Our Future*, Hachette, 2018, pp. 150–61, 75–7; Eduardo Porter, "Is the Populist

Revolt Over? Not If Robots Have Their Way," *New York Times*, January 30, 2018; and Martin Ford, *Rise of the Robots: Technology and the Threat of a Jobless Future*, Basic Books, 2015, pp. 249–52.

3 Data on government debt-to-GDP ratios from IMF, Historical Public Debt Database, 1945–2015, and Global Debt Database, General Government Debt, for 2015–18.

4 See Andrew Glyn, "Social Democracy and Full Employment," Wissenschaftszentrum Berlin für Sozialforschung Discussion Paper, no. FS I 95-302, 1995, p. 10.

5 See Robert Brenner, "What's Good for Goldman Sachs Is Good for America," prologue to the Spanish translation of his *Economics of Global Turbulence*, Akal, 2009; Wolfgang Streeck, "How Will Capitalism End?," *New Left Review*, no. 87, S2, May–June 2014.

6 Emre Tiftik et al., "Global Debt Monitor: Sustainability Matters," Institute of International Finance, January 13, 2020, quoted in John Plender, "The Seeds of the Next Debt Crisis," *Financial Times*, March 3, 2020.

7 Data on economic growth rates from World Bank, *World Development Indicators*, last updated April 2020.

8 Dan McCrum, "Lex in Depth: The Case against Share Buybacks," *Financial Times*, January 29, 2019.

9 John Maynard Keynes, "Economic Possibilities for Our Grandchildren (1930)," in *Essays in Persuasion*, Harcourt Brace, 1932; *The General Theory of Employment, Interest, and Money*, Harcourt, 1964 [1936], pp. 320–6; 374–7. See Geoff Mann, *In the Long Run We Are All Dead: Keynesianism, Political Economy, and Revolution*, Verso, 2017.

10 Keynes, *General Theory*, 376. See also Alvin Hansen, "Economic Progress and Declining Population Growth," *American Economic Review*, vol. 29, no. 1, 1939. For an analysis of the demographic aspects of these arguments, see Melinda Cooper, "Secular Stagnation: Fear of a Non-Reproductive Future," *Postmodern Culture*, vol. 27, no. 1, 2016.

11 Larry Summers, "Demand Side Secular Stagnation," *American Economic Review*, vol. 105, no. 5, 2015, p. 64.

12 Keynes, *General Theory*, p. 324.

13 Keynes, "Economic Possibilities," pp. 368–9.

14 Lorenzo Pecchi and Gustavo Piga, *Revisiting Keynes' Economic Possibilities for our Grandchildren*, MIT Press, 2008. See also Mike Beggs, "Keynes's Jetpack," *Jacobin*, April 17, 2012; Robert Chernomas, "Keynes on Post-Scarcity Society," *Journal of Economic Issues*, vol. 18, no. 4, 1984; James Crotty, *Keynes against Capitalism*, Taylor & Francis, 2019.

15 Robinson admonished the "bastard Keynesians" for inverting the rank order of Keynes's commitments, ventriloquizing Keynes to argue, absurdly, that "if capitalism is incompatible with plenty, plenty ought to be sacrificed to keep capitalism going." See Joan Robinson, "What Has Become of the Keynesian Revolution?," *Challenge*, vol. 6, no. 16, 1974, p. 11.

16 See William Beveridge, *Full Employment in a Free Society*, George Allen & Unwin, 1944, p. 31, 101, 159, 273. In a similar way, the final report of the League of Nations argued that "We must not allow painful memories of the evils of unwanted leisure in the absence of adequate income to blind us to the benefits of wanted leisure for those whose primary material needs have already been assured." See League of Nations, *Economic Stability in the Post-War World: The Conditions of Prosperity after the Transition from War to Peace*, 1945, pp. 228–9.

17 See Robert Pollin, *Greening the Global Economy*, MIT Press, 2015; Ann Pettifor, *The Case for a Green New Deal*, Verso, 2019; and Kate Aronoff et. al., *A Planet to Win: The Case for the Green New Deal*, Verso, 2019. For critiques see Geoff Mann and Joel Wainwright, *Climate Leviathan: A Political Theory of Our Planetary Future*, Verso, 2018, pp. 99–128; Troy Vetesse, "To Freeze the Thames," *New Left Review*, no. 111, S2, May–June 2018; Jason Hickel, "Degrowth: A Theory of Radical Abundance," *Real World Economics Review*, no. 87, 2019, pp. 54–68; and Nicholas Beuret, "A Green New Deal between Whom and for What?," *Viewpoint*, October 24, 2019.

18 See Nixon Apple, "The Rise and Fall of Full Employment Capitalism," *Studies in Political Economy*, vol. 4, no. 1, 1980.

19 For the classic account, see Michal Kalecki, "Political Aspects of Full Employment," *Political Quarterly*, vol. 14, no. 4, 1943. Kalecki was wrong to think that capitalists would oppose full employment as such. They were fine with it, as long as it was achieved via private investment in the course of rapid, export-driven growth. See also Jonathan Levy, "Capital as Process and the History of Capital," *Business History Review*, vol. 91, special issue 3, 2017.

20 See James Crotty, "Post-Keynesian Economic Theory: An Overview and Evaluation," *American Economic Review*, vol. 70, no. 2, 1980, p. 25; Adam Przeworski, "Social Democracy as Historical Phenomenon," *New Left Review*, no. 122, S1, July–August 1980, pp. 56–8.

21 Oskar Lange and Fred M. Taylor, *On the Economic Theory of Socialism*, University of Minnesota Press, 1938, pp. 119–120. Lange suggests that socialists could gain politically by putting forward a "labor plan" to "attack unemployment." However, he cautions, "the great economic power of corporations and banks being what it is, it would be they who would control the public planning authorities rather than the reverse." See pp. 119, 127–129.

22 Thank you to Robert Brenner for helpful comments on this section.

23 See Philippe van Parijs and Yannick Vanderborght, *Basic Income: A Radical Proposal for a Free Society and a Sane Economy*, Harvard University Press, 2017, p. 8; Guy Standing, *Basic Income: A Guide for the Open-Minded*, Yale University Press, 2017. This proposal is discussed in Erik Brynjolfsson and Andrew McAfee, *The Second Machine Age: Work, Progress, and Prosperity in a Time of Brilliant Technologies*, W.W. Norton, 2014, pp. 232–41; Ford, *Rise of the Robots*, pp. 257–9; Stern, *Raising the Floor*, pp. 171–222; and Yang, *War on Normal People*, pp. 165–74.

24 Ishaan Tharoor, "The pandemic strengthens the case for universal basic income," *Washington Post*, April 9, 2020; Sam Meredith, "The coronavirus crisis could pave the way to universal basic

income," *CNBC*, April 16, 2020; Craig Paton, "Coronavirus in Scotland: Nicola Sturgeon eyes plans for universal basic income," *The Times*, May 5, 2020.

25 See James Ferguson, *Give a Man a Fish: Reflections on the New Politics of Distribution*, Duke University Press, 2015.

26 van Parijs and Vanderborght call for a surprisingly exclusionary basic income proposal as a starting point for reform. See ibid., pp. 220–4.

27 This point is recognized in Nick Dyer-Witheford, *Cyber-Proletariat: Global Labour in the Digital Vortex*, Pluto, 2015, pp. 185–6; Nick Srnicek and Alex Williams, *Inventing the Future: Postcapitalism and a World without Work*, Verso, 2015, p. 127; Annie Lowrey, *Give People Money: How UBI Would End Poverty, Revolutionize Work, and Remake the World*, Crown, 2018, p. 130.

28 On Thomas Paine's *Agrarian Justice* (1797), see Van Parijs and Vanderborght, *Basic Income*, pp. 70–2.

29 Milton Friedman, *Capitalism and Freedom*, University of Chicago Press, 1962, pp. 191–5; Friedrich Hayek, *Law, Legislation, and Liberty*, vol. 3, University of Chicago Press, 1979, pp. 54–5.

30 On neoliberalism as a doctrine aimed at constructing markets, rather than freeing them, see Pierre Dardot and Christian Laval, *The New Way of the World: On Neoliberal Society*, Verso, 2013; Quinn Slobodian, *Globalists: The End of Empire and the Birth of Neoliberalism*, Harvard University Press, 2018.

31 Charles Murray, *In Our Hands: A Plan to Replace the Welfare State*, AEI, 2016, pp. 11–15; *Coming Apart*, Crown, 2012. On Murray's intellectual trajectory, see Quinn Slobodian and Stuart Schrader, "The White Man, Unburdened," *Baffler*, no. 40, July 2018. It's striking how many proponents of UBI have been influenced by Murray's work. See Brynjolfsson and McAfee, *Second Machine Age*, pp. 234–7; Ford, *Rise of the Robots*, pp. 262–3; West, *Future of Work*, pp. 99–100; and Lowrey, *Give People Money*, pp. 128–30. Andy Stern narrates a fictional conversation

between Murray and Martin Luther King: *Raising the Floor*, pp. 202–3.

32 Murray, *In Our Hands*, p. xi. See also van Parijs and Vanderborght, *Basic Income*, p. 5, Lowrey, *Give People Money*, pp. 25–6.

33 Murray, *In Our Hands*, pp. 60–8, 81–90.

34 Murray, *In Our Hands*, p. 7. For an astute analysis of the chasm between arguments for income sufficiency and income equality, see Samuel Moyn, *Not Enough: Human Rights in an Unequal World*, Harvard University Press, 2018.

35 van Parijs and Vanderborght, *Basic Income*, p. 214.

36 See ibid., pp. 127–8; Erik Olin Wright, *How to be an Anti-Capitalist in the 21st Century*, Verso, 2019, pp. 74–5; and Srnicek and Williams, *Inventing the Future*, pp. 117–23. For an earlier, influential version of this argument, see Stanley Aronowitz et al., "The Post-work Manifesto," in Stanley Aronowitz and Jonathan Cutler, eds., *Post-work: The Wages of Cybernation*, Routledge, 1998.

37 See Van Parijs and Vanderborght, *Basic Income*, pp. 11–12, 214, 220–4, 127–8. Arguments for voluntary associations and against bureaucracy have been fixtures of council communist and anarcho-syndicalist politics as well. See Immanuel Ness and Dario Azzellini, *Ours to Master and to Own: Workers' Control from the Commune to the Present*, Haymarket, 2011.

38 Srnicek and Williams, *Inventing the Future*, pp. 107–27.

39 Ibid., pp. 117–23. See also Robert J. van der Veen and Philippe van Parijs, "A Capitalist Road to Communism," *Theory and Society*, vol. 15, no. 5, 1986; and Peter Frase, *Four Futures: Life after Capitalism*, Verso, 2016, pp. 54–8.

40 Keynes, "Economic Possibilities," pp. 366–7; West, *Future of Work*, pp. 83–8. See also Manu Saadia, *Trekonomics: The Economics of Star Trek*, Inkshares, 2016; as well as Iain M. Banks's *Culture* series. The popularity of the "fully automated luxury communism" meme speaks to this appealing vision.

41 Alyssa Battistoni, "Alive in the Sunshine," *Jacobin*, January 12, 2014; van Parijs and Vanderborght, *Basic Income*, pp. 227–30.

42 See Elizabeth Anderson, *Private Government: How Employers*

Rule Our Lives (and Why We Don't Talk about It), Princeton University Press, 2017.

43 Katherine Hobson, "Feeling Lonely? Too Much Time on Social Media May Be Why," NPR, March 6, 2017. See also Brian Primack et al., "Social Media Use and Perceived Social Isolation among Young Adults in the US," *American Journal of Preventative Medicine*, vol. 53, no. 1, 2017.

44 See Sareeta Amrute, "Automation Won't Keep Front-Line Workers Safe," *Slate*, April 9, 2020.

45 Meanwhile, the automation theorists could not so much as consider taking control over investment from the capitalists, since they believe their program to rely on private investment in digital technologies.

46 Karl Marx, "Economic and Philosophical Manuscripts (1844)" in Karl Marx, *Early Writings*, Penguin Classics, 1992, p. 327.

47 See Bertram Silverman, "The Rise and Fall of the Swedish Model: Interview with Rudolf Meidner," *Challenge*, vol. 41, no. 1, 1998.

48 See Geoff Eley, *Forging Democracy: The History of the Left in Europe, 1850–2000*, Oxford University Press, 2002, esp. Chs. 10 and 17, on the failure of workers' parties and unions to strike while the iron was hot in post–World War I Germany and Italy and in interwar France.

Chapter 6. Necessity and Freedom

1 Bertolt Brecht, "To Those Born After," in *The Collected Poems of Bertolt Brecht*, Liveright 2018, p. 736.

2 On the limits of actually existing welfare states, as explained by one of their great defenders, see Gøsta Esping-Andersen, *The Three Worlds of Welfare Capitalism*, Princeton University Press, 1990, pp. 9–34.

3 This slogan was emblazoned on the cover of Srnicek and Williams, *Inventing the Future*.

4 See Martin Ford, *Rise of the Robots: Technology and the Threat of*

a Jobless Future, Basic Books, 2015, pp. 246–8; Andrew Yang, *The War on Normal People: The Truth about America's Disappearing Jobs and Why Universal Basic Income Is Our Future*, Hachette, 2018, p. xvii; and Peter Frase, *Four Futures: Life after Capitalism*, Verso, 2016, pp. 48–9. For an extended discussion, see Manu Saadia, *Trekonomics: The Economics of Star Trek*, Inkshares, 2016, pp. 65–86. This vision may have found its inspiration in the USSR. In 1961, Khrushchev called for communism in twenty years. The Strugatsky brothers, a sci-fi duo, penned a series of incredible short stories in response entitled *Noon: 22nd Century* (Macmillan, 1978 [1961]), describing space exploration in a communist future. Alongside their later novel, *Hard to Be a God* (Eyre Methuen, 1975 [1964]), this vision of space-faring communists perhaps served as a model for *Star Trek* and for Banks's *Culture* series, both of which premiered in 1987.

5 Thomas More, *Utopia*, 2nd ed., Yale University Press, 2014, pp. 47, 132.

6 For Hammond's 1858 mudsill theory, which claimed it was necessary to have slaves for drudgery, so the rest of society could be raised above the muck, see Elizabeth Anderson, *Private Government*, Princeton University Press, 2017, pp. 30–1. See also W.E.B. Du Bois, *Darkwater: Voices from within the Veil*, Dover, 1999 [1920], p. 69.

7 See More, *Utopia*, pp. 60–72; Étienne Cabet, *Travels in Icaria*, Syracuse University Press, 2003 [1840], pp. 80–9; Karl Marx, *Grundrisse: Foundations of a Critique of Political Economy*, Penguin, 1993, pp. 707–12; Karl Marx, *Capital*, vol. 3, Penguin, 1991, pp. 958–9; and Peter Kropotkin, *The Conquest of Bread*, Cambridge University Press, 2015, pp. 99–112. For a general discussion, which, however, excludes Cabet and Kropotkin, see Edward Granter, *Critical Theory and the End of Work*, Ashgate, 2009, esp. pp. 31–67. Here I leave to one side thinkers like Charles Fourier, William Morris, and Herbert Marcuse, who essentially suggested that the collapse of spheres could be achieved by turning all work into play. Single-realm conceptions of a post-scarcity world are, in

my view, both totalitarian and hopelessly utopian (in the bad sense of the term).

8 Quoted in Marx, *Capital*, vol. 1, p. 532. See also William Booth, "The New Household Economy," *American Political Science Review*, vol. 85, no. 1, March 1991, pp. 59–75; and Claudio Katz, "The Socialist Polis: Antiquity and Socialism in Marx's Thought," *Review of Politics*, vol. 56, no. 2, 1994, pp. 237–60.

9 More, *Utopia*, pp. 75–9 (on the slaves' "golden chains"); 117 (on the early Christians); 47 (on the abolition of money and private property); 19–25 (on the enclosures); 66 (on freedom). Marx obliquely references More's "golden chains" in *Capital*. See Marx, *Capital*, vol. 1, p. 769. On More as a precursor to Marx, see William Morris, "Foreword to Thomas More's Utopia" [1893], in William Morris, *News from Nowhere and Other Writings*, Penguin Classics, 1993, pp. 371–5.

10 See Robert Sutton, "Introduction," in Cabet, *Travels in Icaria*, p. x.

11 See David Gregory, "Karl Marx's and Friedrich Engels' Knowledge of French Socialism in 1842–43," *Historical Reflections*, vol. 10, no. 1, Spring 1983, pp. 143–93; and Bruno Liepold, "Citizen Marx: The Relationship between Karl Marx and Republicanism," PhD Diss., University of Oxford, 2017.

12 Frank Manuel and Fritzie Manuel, *Utopian Thought in the Western World*, Harvard University Press, 1979, p. 712.

13 See Paul Corcoran, ed., *Before Marx: Socialism and Communism in France*, Macmillan, 1983. Marx confronted two related tendencies, which might have led him astray in the course of his political development. On the one hand, the automation theorists of his time—Etzler, Ure, and Babbage—claimed that machines were already substituting for human labor, making possible the abolition of necessity as such, and through it, the creation of a world of fully free individuality—a position that Marx rejected. On the other hand, Fourierists imagined that in a postcapitalist society, work could be transformed into play, thereby absorbing necessity into freedom. Marx rejected this

communitarian position as well, claiming, against Fourier, that necessity could be taken under collective care and control but not resolved into play. Keeping the realms of freedom and necessity separate made Marx a Morist.

14 See Karl Marx and V.I. Lenin, *The Civil War in France: The Paris Commune*, International Publishers, 1989 [1871]; and Raya Dunayevskaya, *Marxism and Freedom*, Humanity Books, 2000, pp. 92–102.

15 Kristin Ross, *Communal Luxury: The Political Imaginary of the Paris Commune*, Verso, 2015, pp. 91–116.

16 See Otto Neurath, "Through War Economy to Economy in Kind" in Marie Neurath and Robert Cohen, eds., *Otto Neurath: Empiricism and Sociology*, D. Reidel Publishing, 1973; Du Bois, *Darkwater*, pp. 56–9, 69; John Dewey, *Liberalism and Social Action*, Prometheus, 2000 [1935], pp. 37–60; Karl Polanyi, *The Great Transformation*, Beacon, 2001 [1944], pp. 257–68. See also Marcel van der Linden, "The Prehistory of Post-Scarcity Anarchism: Josef Weber and the Movement for a Democracy of Content (1947–1964)," *Anarchist Studies*, no. 9, 2001, pp. 127–45. The socialist calculation debate, initiated by Ludwig von Mises in 1920, condemned socialism for, in Mises's view, being unable to offer a rational basis on which to choose between different methods of production, especially when it came to the production of goods that were themselves inputs into other production processes.

17 Edward Bellamy, *Looking Backward, 2000–1887*, Oxford, 2007 [1888], pp. 39–44.

18 "Putting an end to garbage collection as a job some have to do for years, will be a lot more than job rotation: it will imply changes in the process and logic of garbage *creation* and disposal": Gilles Dauvé, *Eclipse and Re-Emergence of the Communist Movement*, PM Press, 2015, p. 54.

19 Ross, *Communal Luxury*, is evocative of a form of "luxury communism" that need not be "fully automated."

20 See James Klagge, "Marx's Realms of Freedom and Necessity,"

Canadian Journal of Philosophy, vol. 16, no. 4, 1986, pp. 769–78.

21 More, *Utopia*, pp. 67–8. See also Kropotkin, *Conquest of Bread*, pp. 58–63.

22 James Boggs, "The American Revolution" (1963), in Stephen Ward, ed., *Pages from a Black Radical's Notebook: A James Boggs Reader*, Wayne State University Press, 2011, p. 110.

23 More, *Utopia*, p. 130.

24 On this point, see Part 2 of Martin Hägglund, *This Life: Secular Faith and Spiritual Freedom*, Pantheon, 2019, especially pp. 221–37 and 301–25, where Hägglund develops an account of the place of the realms of necessity and freedom in democratic socialism that is similar to my account of their place in a post-scarcity world.

25 Saadia, *Trekonomics*, p. 40.

26 Kropotkin, *Conquest of Bread*, pp. 138–9.

27 Daniel Pink, *Drive: The Surprising Truth about What Motivates Us*, Riverhead, 2009.

28 See John O'Neill, *The Market: Ethics, Knowledge, and Politics*, Routledge, 1998; Daniel Saros, *Information Technology and Socialist Construction*, Routledge, 2014; and Evgeny Morozov, "Digital Socialism?," *New Left Review* 116/117, S2, March–June 2019. I am grateful to Björn Westergard for his generous assistance in helping me understand these issues and for pointing me toward possible solutions. See Björn Westergard, "Review: *People's Republic of Walmart*," *The Machinery Question*, August 28, 2019, available at machineryquesiton.com.

29 In that sense, "equality enables—rather than detracts from—individualism": Ross, *Communal Luxury*, p. 108. See also More, *Utopia*, pp. 61–2; Marx, *Grundrisse*, pp. 711–12; Marx, *Capital*, vol. 1, pp. 532–3; and Kropotkin, *Conquest of Bread*, pp. 99–112.

30 Theodor Adorno, *Minima Moralia: Reflections from Damaged Life*, Verso, 2005, p. 157.

31 In a world without scarcity, people have the chance to exit from oppression back into freedom. "If I am tormented in one place, who will keep me from going someplace else?" J.J. Rousseau, *The*

Discourses and Other Early Political Writings, Cambridge University Press, 1997, p. 158. See also Cory Doctorow, *Walkaway*, Tor, 2017.

32 See Stanley Aronowitz et al., "The Post-Work Manifesto," in Stanley Aronowitz and Jonathan Cutler, eds., *Post-Work: The Wages of Cybernation*, London 1998.

33 Saadia, *Trekonomics*, p. 61.

34 Michael Lebowitz, *The Socialist Alternative: Real Human Development*, Monthly Review, 2010, pp. 31–45.

35 For an account of utopia amid scarcity, see Ursula K. Le Guin, *The Dispossessed: An Ambiguous Utopia*, HarperCollins, 1994, as well as Fredric Jameson's commentary on "world reduction" in Le Guin's novels in *Archeologies of the Future: The Desire Called Utopia and Other Science Fictions*, Verso, 2007, pp. 267–80. See also Frase, *Four Futures*, pp. 91–119.

36 Most UBI theorists end up admitting this point. See, for example, Philippe van Parijs and Yannick Vanderborght, *Basic Income: A Radical Proposal for a Free Society and a Sane Economy*, Harvard University Press, 2017, p. 246.

Postscript: Agents of Change

1 Robert J. van der Veen and Philippe van Parijs, "A Capitalist Road to Communism," *Theory and Society*, vol. 15, no. 5, 1986, pp. 652–3; Nick Srnicek and Alex Williams, *Inventing the Future: Postcapitalism and a World without Work*, Verso, 2015, pp. 9–13. Less radical automation theorists are not only dismissive of social struggles, but hostile to them. Andrew Yang claims that the only such struggle possible today is one "born of race and identity with automation-driven economics as the underlying force." He lays out a terrifying vision in which truck drivers, facing up to their own technological obsolescence, organize to blockade roads, inspiring, in turn, mass shootings, anti-tax revolts, the spread of anti-Semitic viral videos, and the rise of an ethnonationalist party advocating a return to a simpler life under a

racial state. See Andrew Yang, *The War on Normal People: The Truth about America's Disappearing Jobs and Why Universal Basic Income Is Our Future*, Hachette, 2018, pp. 158–9.

2 Wolfgang Streeck, "How Will Capitalism End?," *New Left Review*, no. 87, S2, May–June 2014, p. 48.

3 Among texts that attempt to take stock of these movements as a whole, see Paul Mason, *Why It's Still Kicking Off Everywhere: The New Global Revolutions*, Verso, 2013; Manuel Castells, *Networks of Outrage and Hope: Social Movements in the Internet Age*, 2nd ed., Wiley, 2015; Endnotes, "The Holding Pattern," *Endnotes*, no. 3, 2013; and Göran Therborn, "New Masses?," *New Left Review*, no. 85, S2, Jan.–Feb. 2014. On the 2019 wave, see Jack Shenker, "This Wave of Global Protest Is Being Led by the Children of the Financial Crash," *Guardian*, October 29, 2019 and Robin Wright, "The Story of 2019: Protests in Every Corner of the Globe," *New Yorker*, December 31, 2019.

4 Paul Mason, *Postcapitalism: A Guide to Our Future*, FSG, 2015, p. 29.

5 See Gay Seidman, *Manufacturing Militance: Workers' Movements in Brazil and South Africa, 1970–1985*, UC Press, 1994.

6 See, for example, Kim Moody, *On New Terrain: How Capital Is Reshaping the Battleground of Class War*, Haymarket, 2017.

7 See Federico Rossi, *The Poor's Struggle for Political Incorporation: The Piquetero Movement in Argentina*, Cambridge University Press, 2017.

Index

Adorno, Theodor, 90
Africa. *See also* South Africa
  expansion of nonstandard
    employment in, 54
  unemployment benefits in, 122n27
  universal basic income (UBI) and,
    72
agents of change, 95–9
agriculture
  overcapacity in, 37–8
  production and, 23–4
  role of technology in, 41
AI (artificial intelligence), 7, 40,
  116n35
Algeria, waves of strikes in, 96
apparel industry, 42–3
Argentina
  employment rates in, 53
  piquetero movement, 98
  waves of strikes in, 96
Aristotle, 83, 84
artificial intelligence (AI), 7, 40,
  116n35
Asia
  capital accumulation in, 43
  deindustrialization in, 21
  employment landscape in, 50
  expansion of nonstandard
    employment in, 54

job security in, 52–3
asymptomatic stagnation,
  123–4n40
Australia, waves of strikes in, 96
Austria, out-of-work income
  maintenance/support in,
  119–20n6
automation discourse
  about, ix–x, xi–xiii, 1–2
  fears of, 5–8
  labor undemand, 8–13
  periodicity of, 8
  principle propositions of, 2
  solutions for, 65–6
automation technologies, 5–6
Autor, David, 9, 61

Babbage, Charles, 133–4n13
  *On the Economy of Machinery and
    Manufactures,* 7–8
Babeuf, François-Noël, 85
Bangladesh, sewbots in, 43
Bank of Japan, 37
Banks, Iain M., 130n40
  Culture series, 3, 130n40, 132n4
Bastani, Aaron, 5
Baumol, William, 57, 59–60,
  123–4n40, 124n41
Bell, Daniel, 57